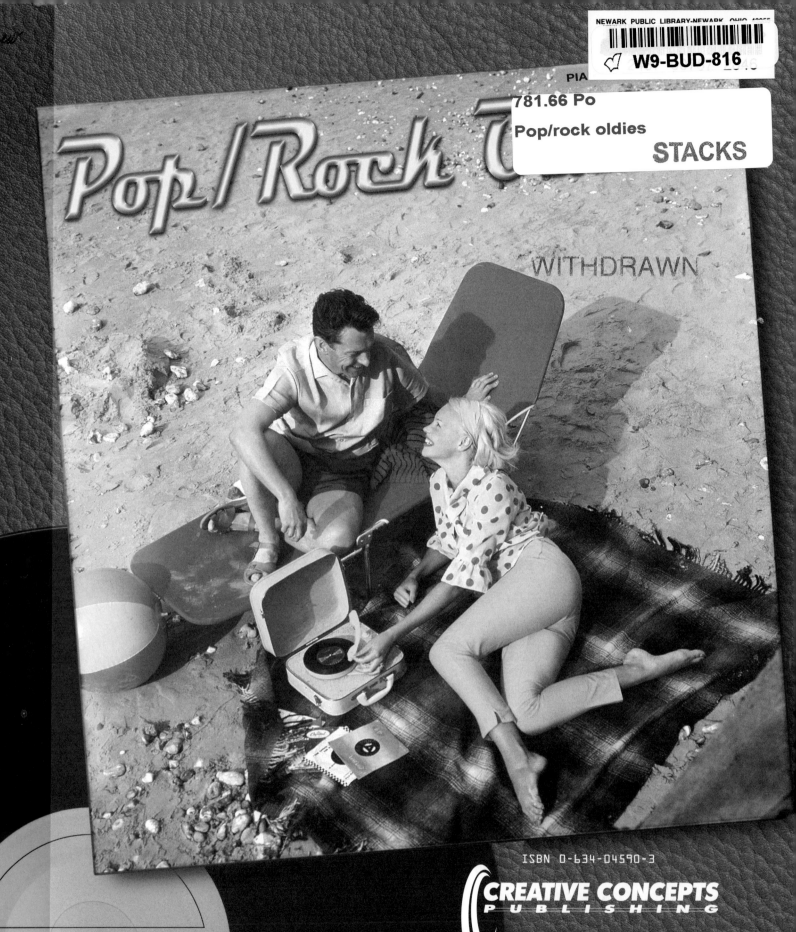

WITHDRAWN

ISBN 0-634-04590-3

CREATIVE CONCEPTS
P U B L I S H I N G

EXCLUSIVELY DISTRIBUTED BY

HAL•LEONARD®
CORPORATION
7777 W. BLUEMOUND RD. P.O. BOX 13819 MILWAUKEE, WI 53213

RPM   315343

POP/ROCK OLDIES
– Various Artists –

C O N T E N T S

AHAB THE ARAB

Words and Music by
RAY STEVENS

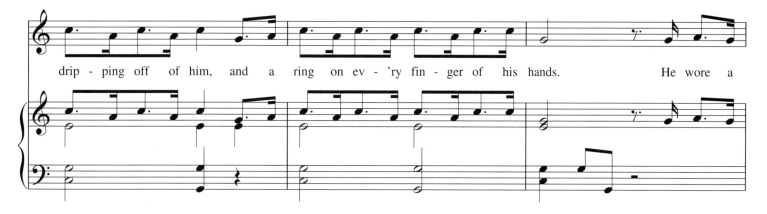

dripping off of him, and a ring on ev-'ry fin-ger of his hands. He wore a

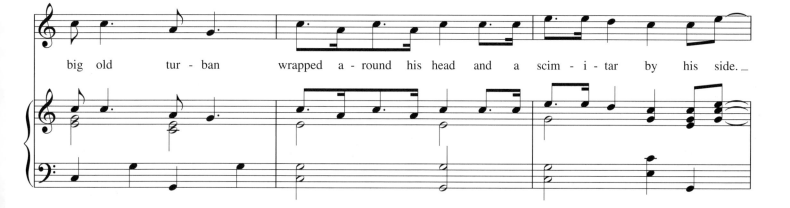

big old tur-ban wrapped a-round his head and a scim-i-tar by his side.

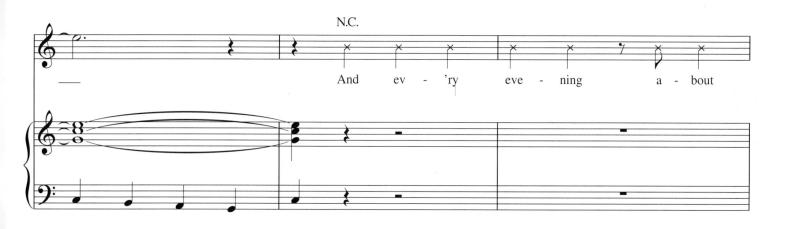

And ev-'ry eve-ning a-bout

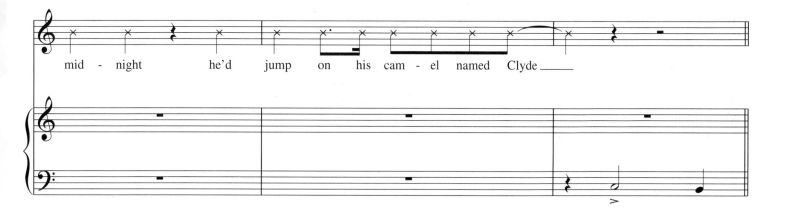

mid-night he'd jump on his cam-el named Clyde

(Spoken:)
and ride through the night to the Sultan's tent where he would secretly meet up with Fatima of the seven veils, the swingingest number one dancer in the Sultan's whole harem, 'cause like him and her had a thing going. You know, they'd been carrying on for some time now behind the Sultan's back and you could hear him talk to his camel. As he rode out across the dunes, his voice would cut through the still night desert air and he'd say, (imitate Arabian speech) which is Arabic for, "Whoa, babies." And Clyde would say, (imitate camel voice). Well, he

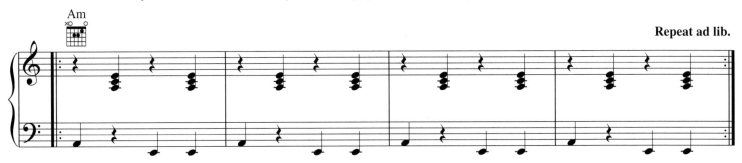

brought his camel to a screeching halt at the rear of Fatima's tent, jumped off Clyde, snuck around the corner and into the tent he went. There he saw Fatima lying on a zebra skin rug, wearing rings on her fingers and bells on her toes and a bone in her nose. Ho, ho.

There she was, friends and neighbors, lying there in all her radiant beauty, eating on a raisin and a grape and an apricot and a pomegranate and a bowl of chitterlings, two bananas, three Hershey bars, and sipping an R-ER-C coke cola, listening to her transistor, watching "The Grand Old Opry" and reading Mad *magazine while she sang, "Does your chewing gum lose its flavor?" And Ahab walked up to her and he said, (imitate Arabian speech) which is Arabic for, "Let's twist again like we did last summer, babies." And she said, (coy, girlish laugh) "Crazy baby." 'Round and around and around and around, etc. And that's the story 'bout*

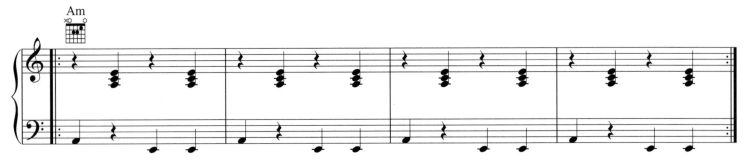

A - hab, the A - rab, the sheik of the burn - ing sand.

CRIMSON AND CLOVER

Words and Music by TOMMY JAMES
and PETER LUCIA

Crim - son and clo - ver, o - ver and o - ver. Crim - son and clo - ver,

o - ver and o - ver.

BE-BOP-A-LULA

Words and Music by TEX DAVIS
and GENE VINCENT

Be - bop - a - lu - la, she's my ba - by. Be - bop - a - lu - la, I don't mean may - be.

Be - bop - a - lu - la, she's my ba - by. Be - bop - a - lu - la, I don't mean may - be.

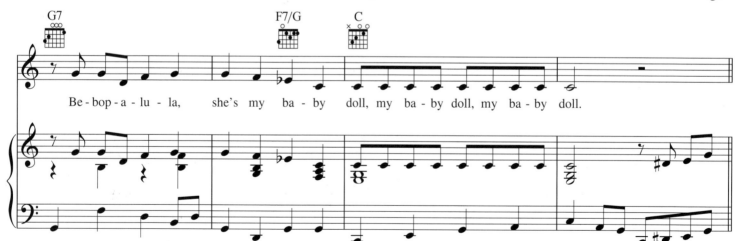

Be - bop - a - lu - la, she's my ba - by doll, my ba - by doll, my ba - by doll.

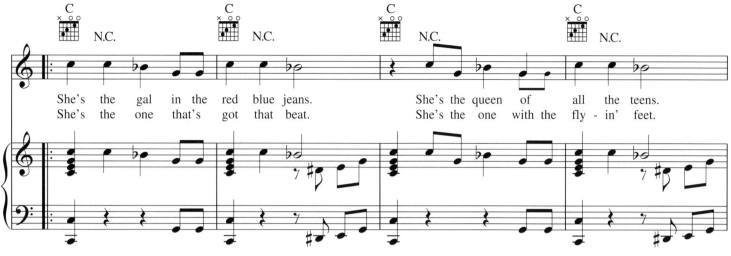

She's the gal in the red blue jeans.
She's the one that's got that beat.

She's the queen of all the teens.
She's the one with the fly - in' feet.

She's the one _____ that I know.
She's the one that walks a - round the store.

She's the one that loves me so.
She's the one that gets more and more.

Be - bop - a - lu - la, she's my ba - by. Be - bop - a - lu - la, I don't mean may - be.

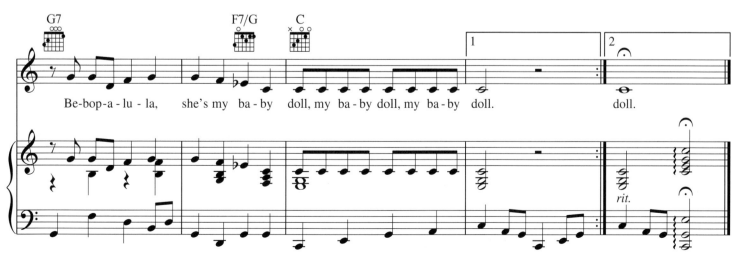

Be - bop - a - lu - la, she's my ba - by doll, my ba - by doll, my ba - by doll.

doll.

rit.

THE BOY FROM NEW YORK CITY

Words and Music by JOHN TAYLOR
and GEORGE DAVIS

Moderate and very steady

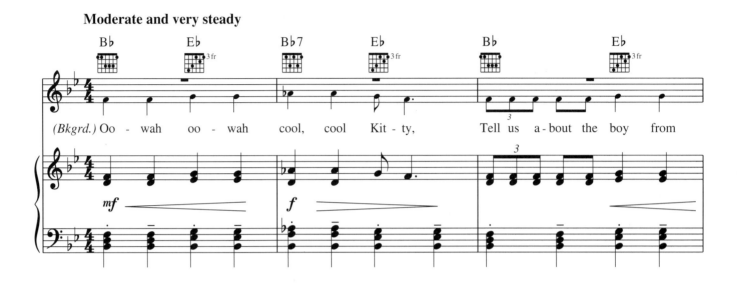

(Bkgrd.) Oo - wah oo - wah cool, cool Kit - ty, Tell us a - bout the boy from

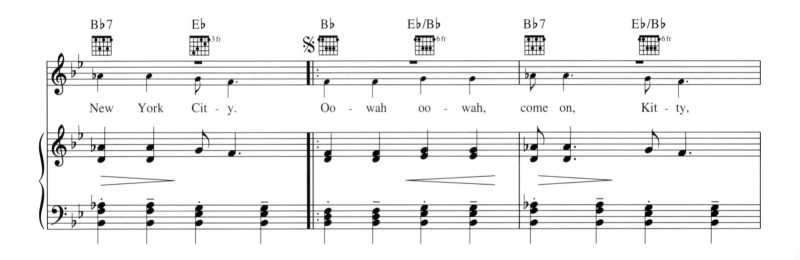

New York Cit - y. Oo - wah oo - wah, come on, Kit - ty,

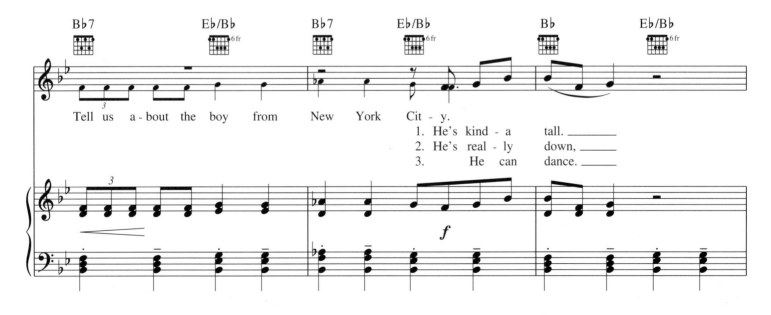

Tell us a - bout the boy from New York Cit - y.
1. He's kind - a tall. _____
2. He's real - ly down, _____
3. He can dance. _____

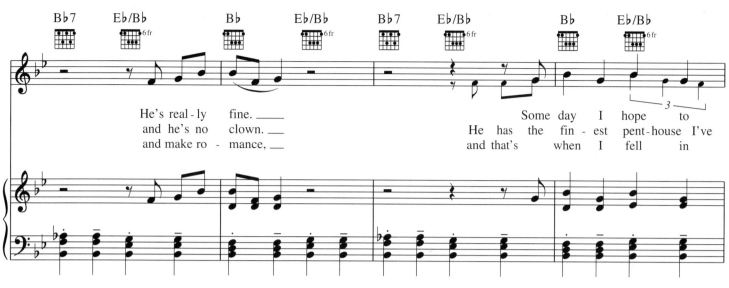

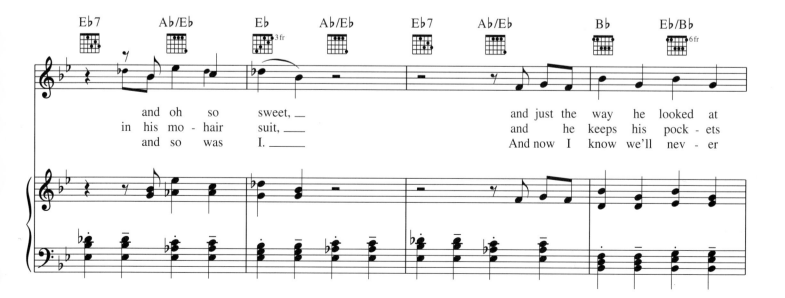

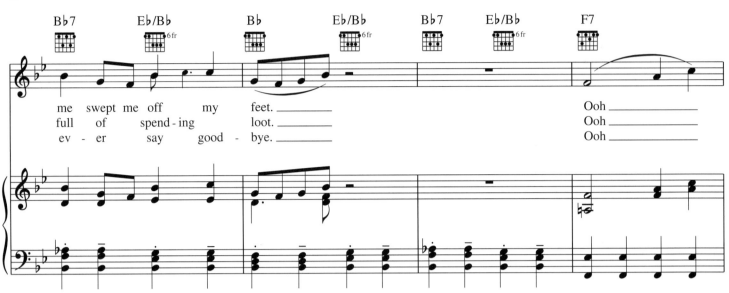

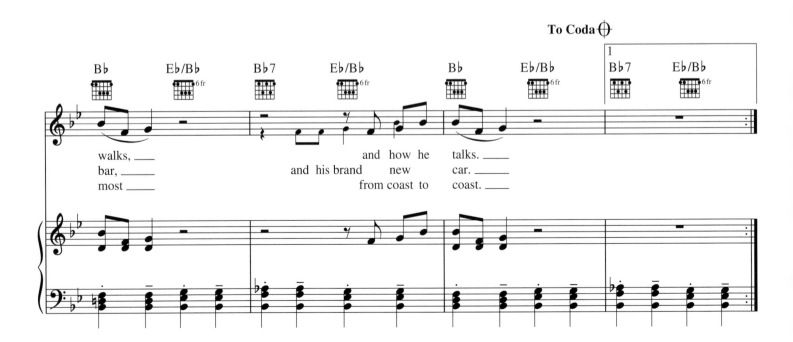

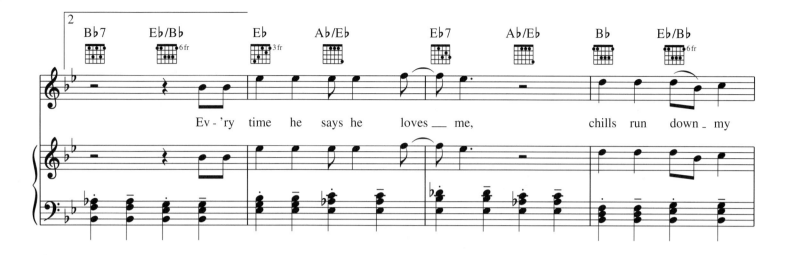

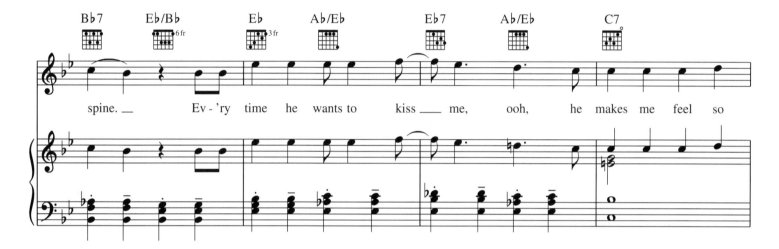

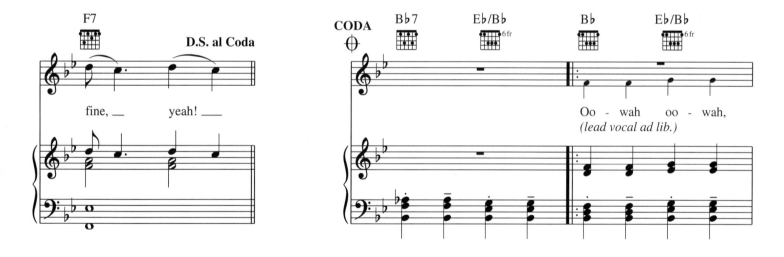

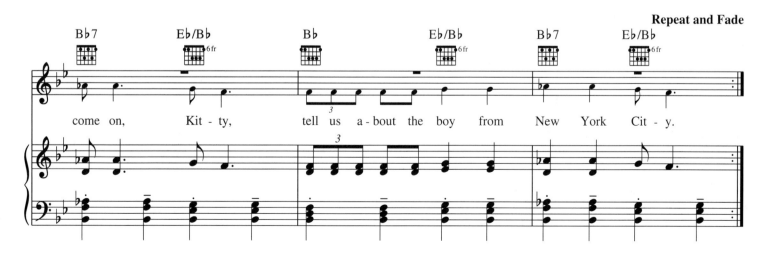

CALIFORNIA SUN

Words and Music by MORRIS LEVY
and HENRY GLOVER

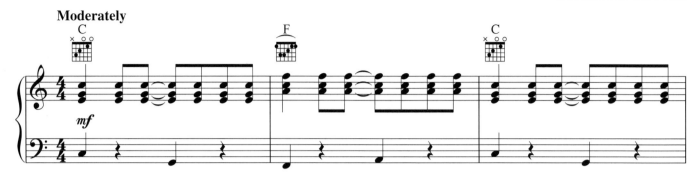

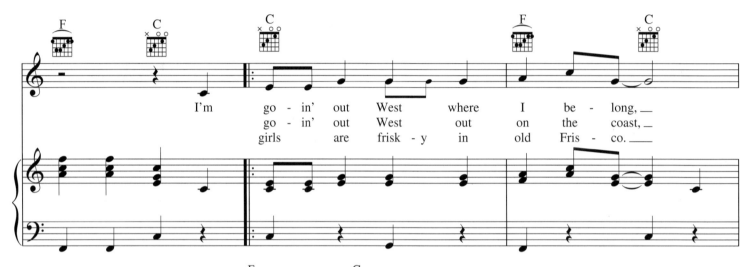

I'm go - in' out West where I be - long, __
go - in' out West out on the coast, __
girls are frisk - y in old Fris - co. __

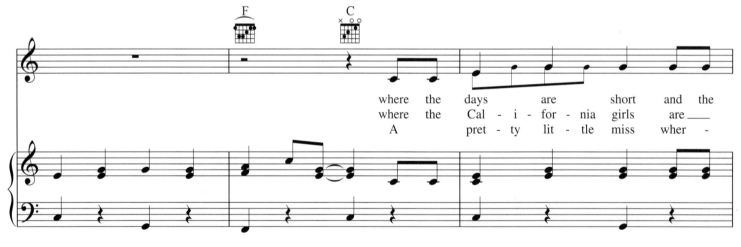

where the days are short and the
where the Cal - i - for - nia girls are __
A pret - ty lit - tle miss wher -

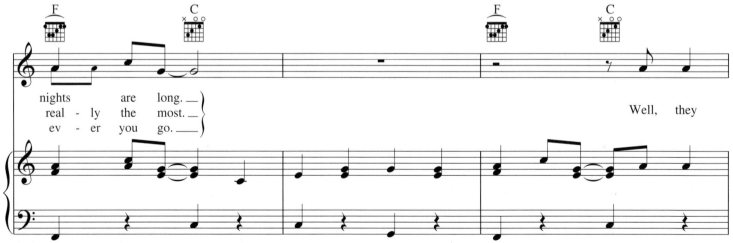

nights are long. __
real - ly the most. __
ev - er you go. __

Well, they

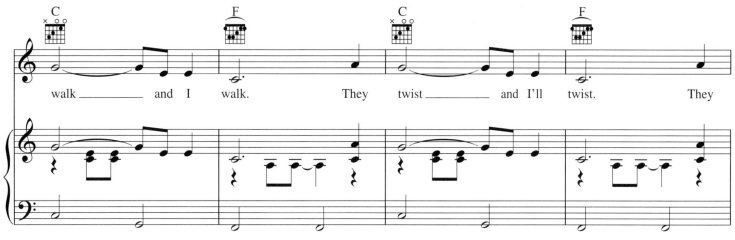

walk _____ and I walk. They twist _____ and I'll twist. They

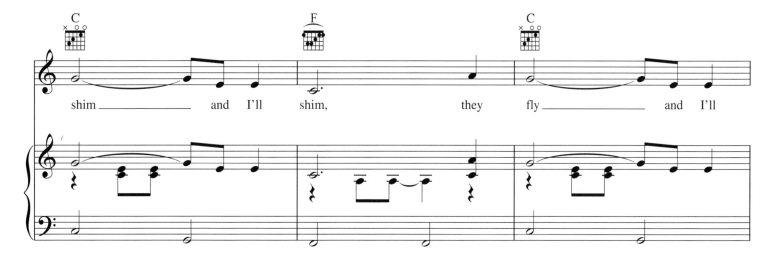

shim _____ and I'll shim, they fly _____ and I'll

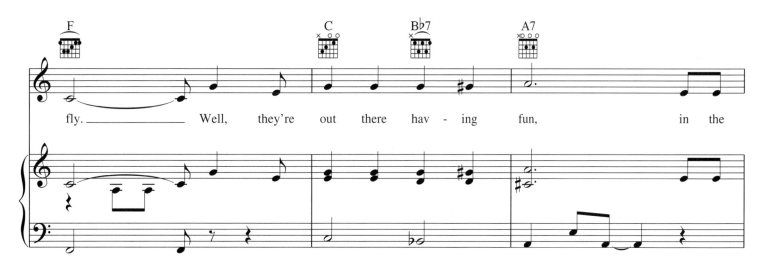

fly. _____ Well, they're out there hav - ing fun, in the

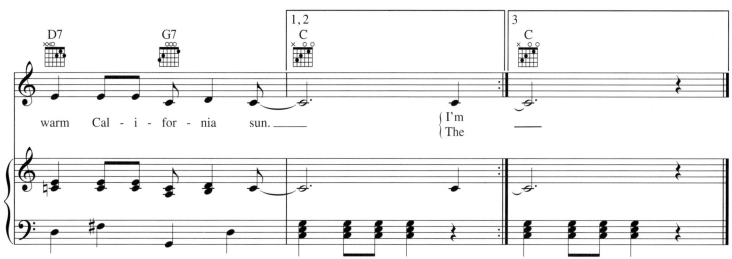

warm Cal - i - for - nia sun. _____ { I'm { The _____

DADDY'S HOME

Words and Music by JAMES SHEPPARD
and WILLIAM H. MILLER

22

DIZZY

Words and Music by TOMMY ROE
and FREDDY WELLER

DONNA

Words and Music by
RITCHIE VALENS

Oh, Don - na, oh, Don - na,

oh, Don - na, oh, Don - na.

I had a girl, _____ Don - na _____ was her name,
Now that you're gone, _____ I'm left _____ all a - lone,

since she left me _____ I've nev - er _____ been the same, _____ } 'Cause I
all by my - self _____ to wan - der _____ and _____ roam, _____

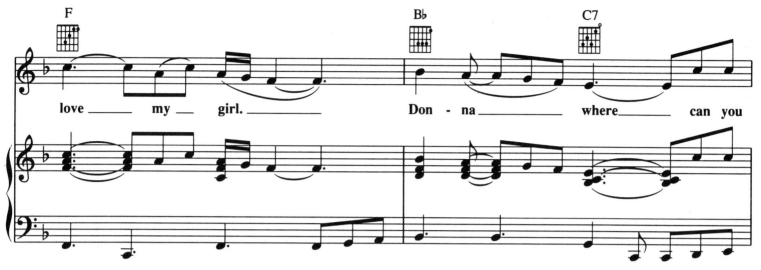

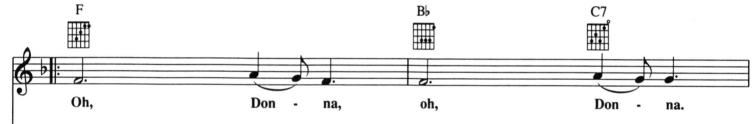

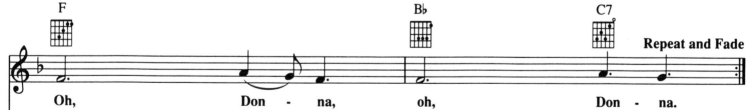

GEE WHIZ

Words and Music by
CARLA THOMAS

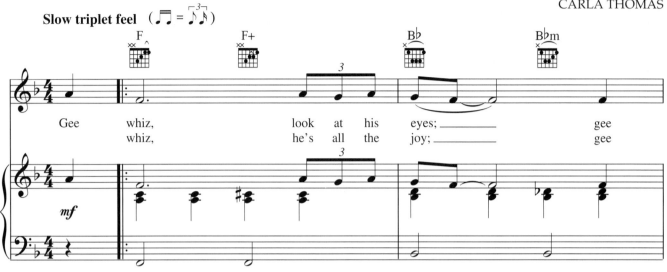

Gee whiz, look at his eyes; _____ gee
whiz, he's all the joy; _____ gee

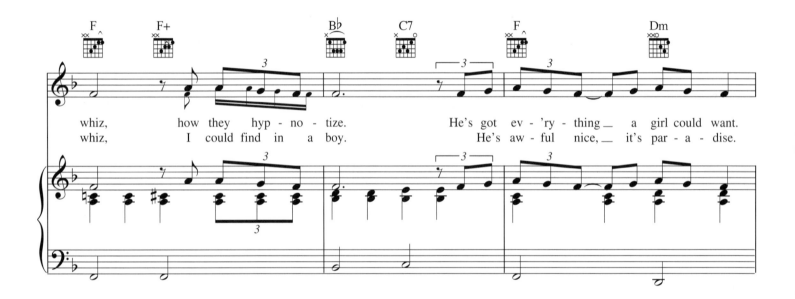

whiz, how they hyp - no - tize. He's got ev - 'ry - thing ___ a girl could want.
whiz, I could find in a boy. He's aw - ful nice, ___ it's par - a - dise.

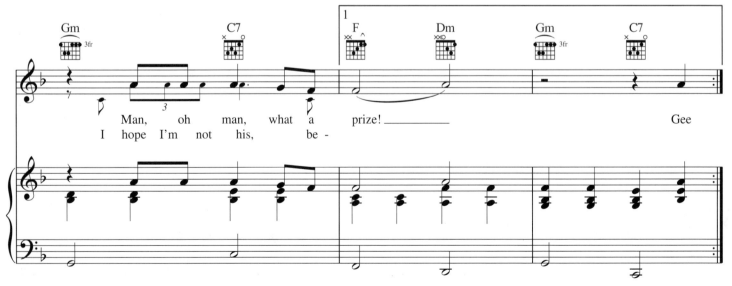

Man, oh man, what a prize! _____ Gee
I hope I'm not his, be -

cause: _____ Heav - en up a - bove

knows how much __ I love that fel - low so.

An - gels sing _____ of the love I _____ bring; I

hope our love will grow and grow. Oh, __ gee whiz, I love that

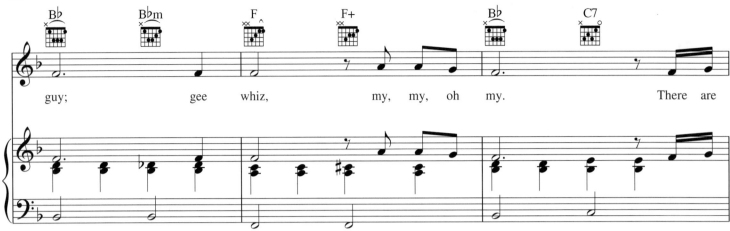

guy; gee whiz, my, my, oh my. There are

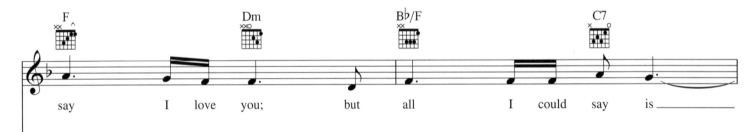

things we could do, I could

say I love you; but all I could say is ____

gee whiz. ____

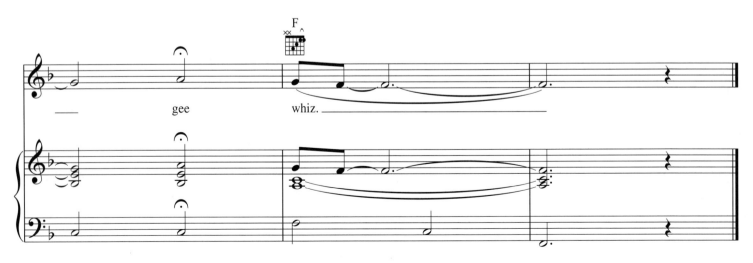

GOOD VIBRATIONS

Words and Music by BRIAN WILSON
and MIKE LOVE

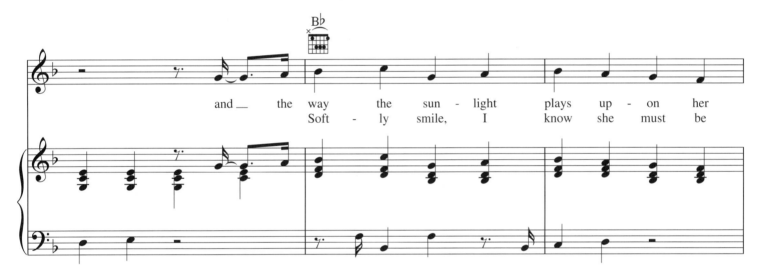

gen - tle word _____ on ___ the wind that lifts her
in her eyes, _____ she ___ goes with me to a

per - fume through the air. _____)
blos - som world. _____)

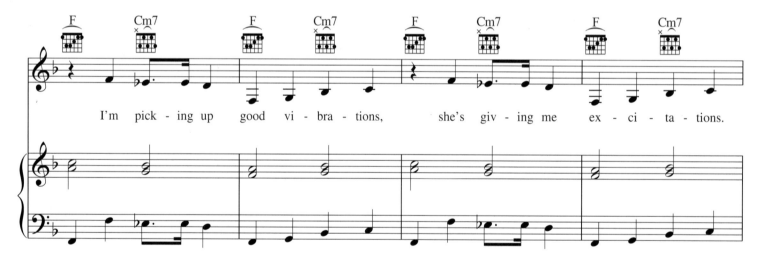

I'm pick - ing up good vi - bra - tions, she's giv - ing me ex - ci - ta - tions.

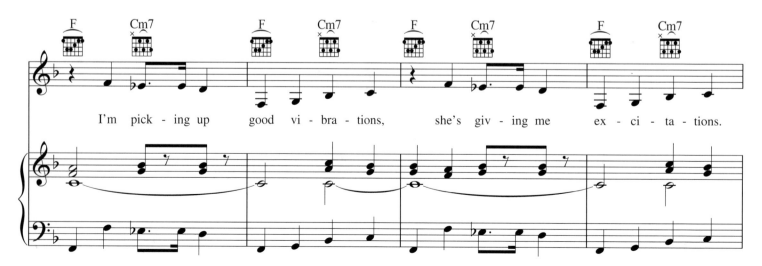

I'm pick - ing up good vi - bra - tions, she's giv - ing me ex - ci - ta - tions.

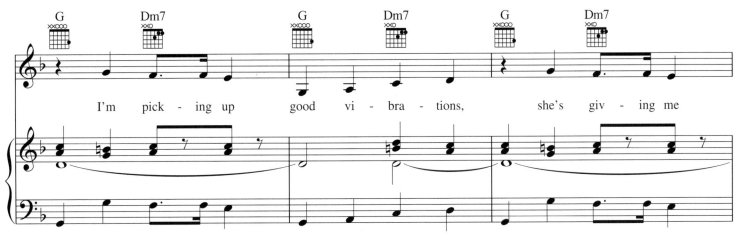

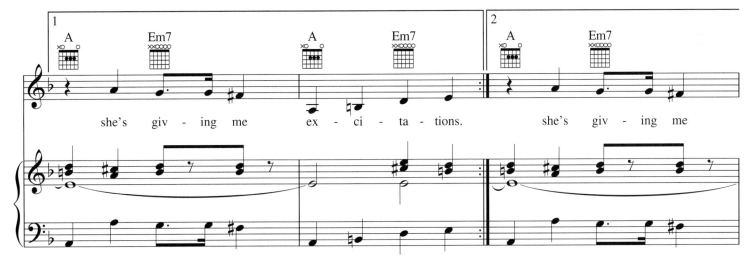

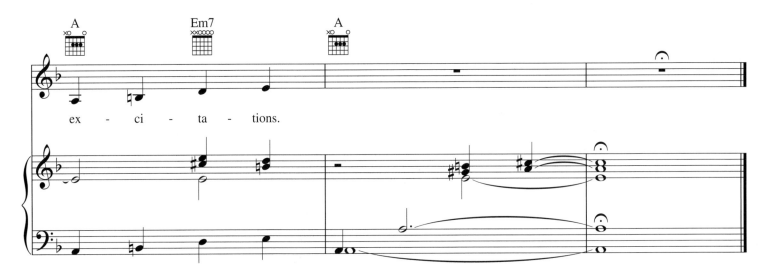

GOD ONLY KNOWS

Words and Music by BRIAN WILSON
and TONY ASHER

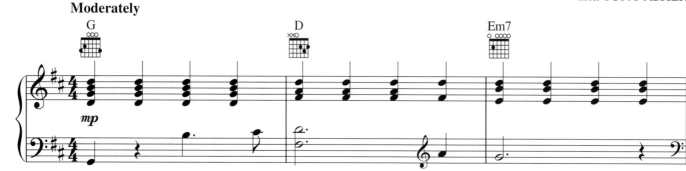

I may not al - ways love you,
If you should ev - er leave me,

but long as there are _____ stars ___ a - bove you, ___
oh, life would still go _____ on, ___ be - lieve me. ___

you'll nev - er need to doubt __ it. ___
The world could show noth - ing to _____ me, ___

I'll make you so
so what good would

GOODNIGHT MY LOVE, PLEASANT DREAMS

Words and Music by GEORGE MOTOLA
and JOHN MARASCALCO

Good-night my love, pleas-ant dreams and sleep tight, my love.

May to-mor-row be sun-ny and bright and bring you clos-er to

me. _____ Be-fore you go,

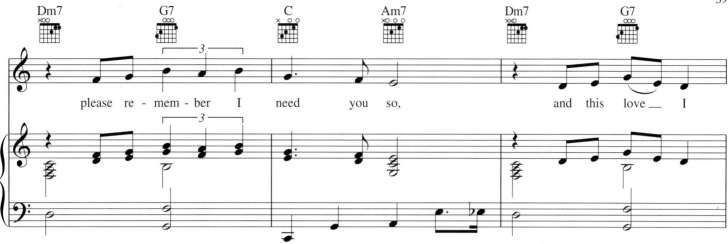

please re - mem - ber I need you so, and this love __ I

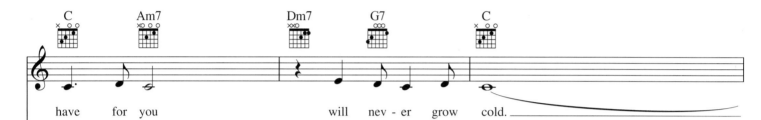

have for you will nev - er grow cold. _____

If you __ should a - wake __ in the still __ of the night,

please have no fear. Just __ close your eyes, then

you'll ___ re - al - ize that my love will watch o - ver you, dear, al - ways.

Good - night my love, pleas - ant dreams and sleep tight, my love.

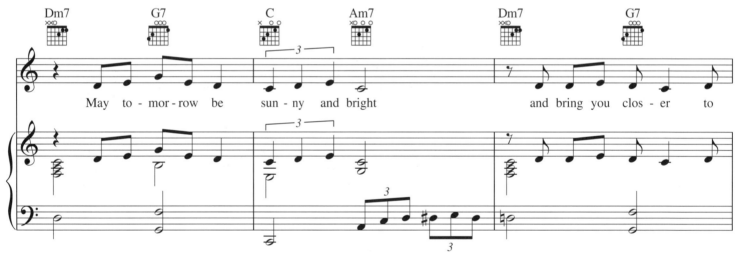

May to - mor - row be sun - ny and bright and bring you clos - er to

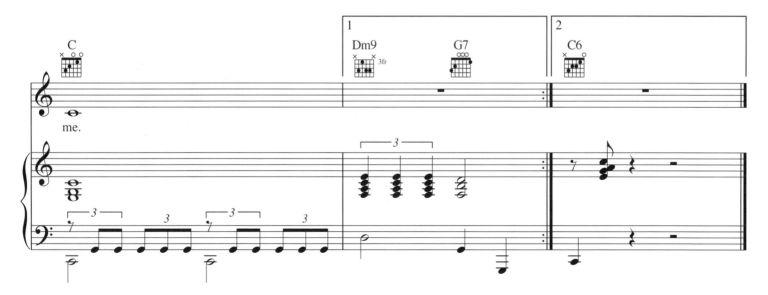

me.

I LIKE IT LIKE THAT

Words and Music by
CHRIS KENNER

HOLD ON I'M COMIN'

Words and Music by ISAAC HAYES
and DAVID PORTER

Moderately, with a strong beat

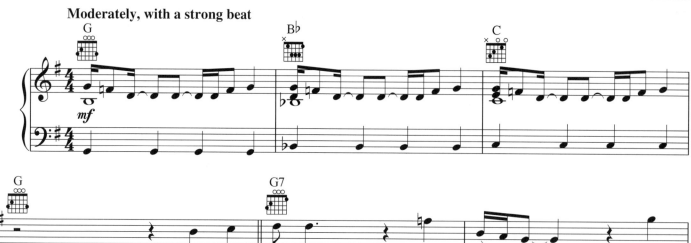

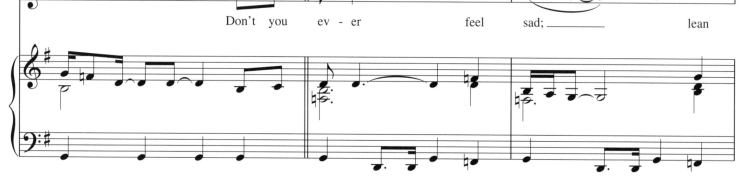

Don't you ev-er feel sad; _____ lean

on me when times _____ are bad. _____ When the day _____

_____ comes and you're down _____ in a riv-er of trou-ble and I got to

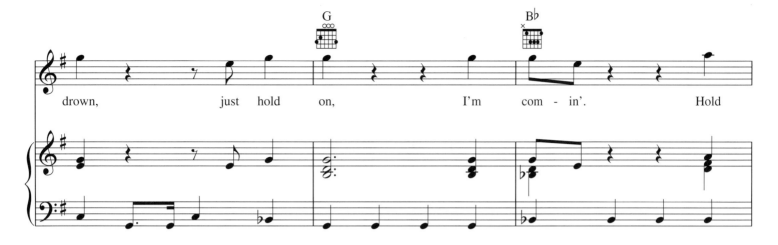

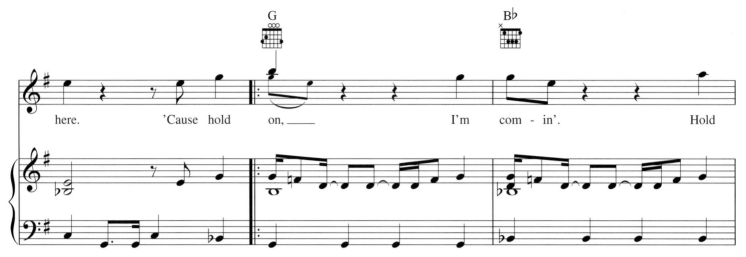

here. 'Cause hold on, _____ I'm com - in'. Hold

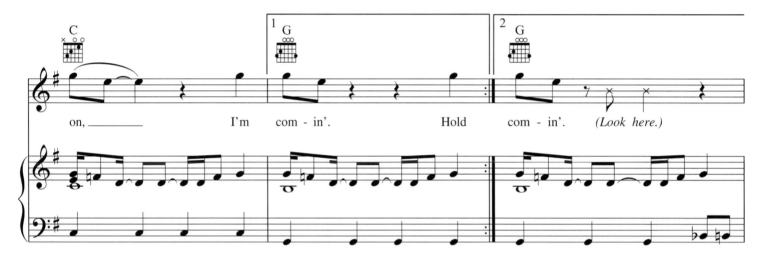

on, _____ I'm com - in'. Hold com - in'. *(Look here.)*

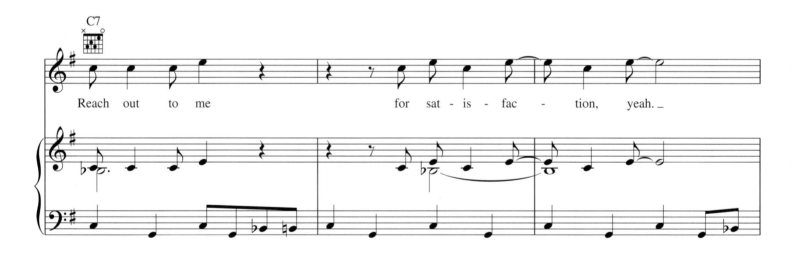

Reach out to me for sat - is - fac - tion, yeah. _

Call my name, _ now, for quick re - ac -

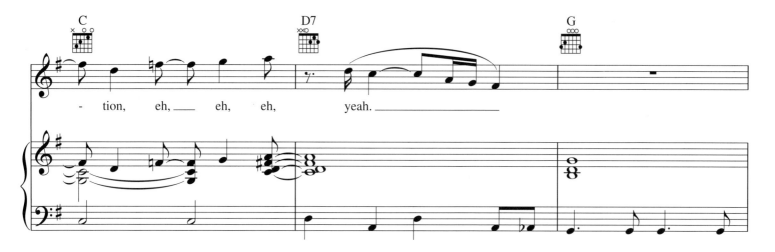

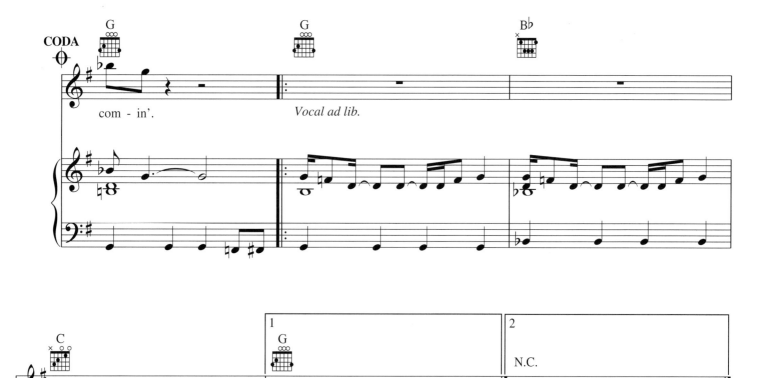

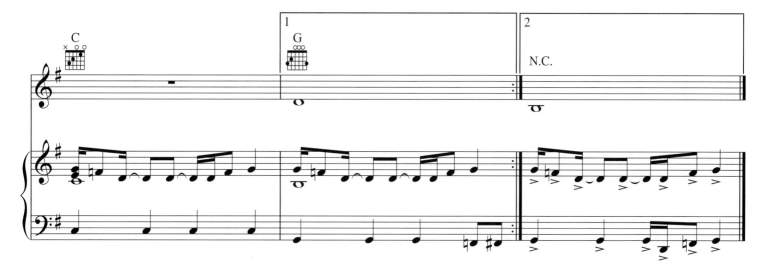

I FOUGHT THE LAW

Words and Music by
SONNY CURTIS

I THINK WE'RE ALONE NOW

Words and Music by
RITCHIE CORDELL

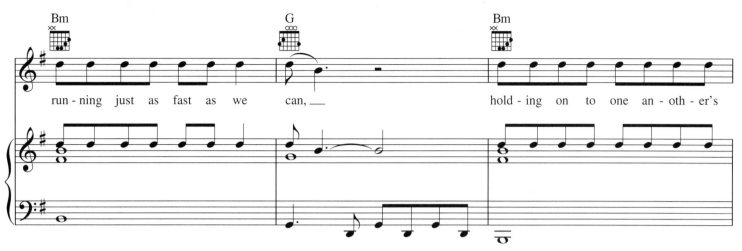

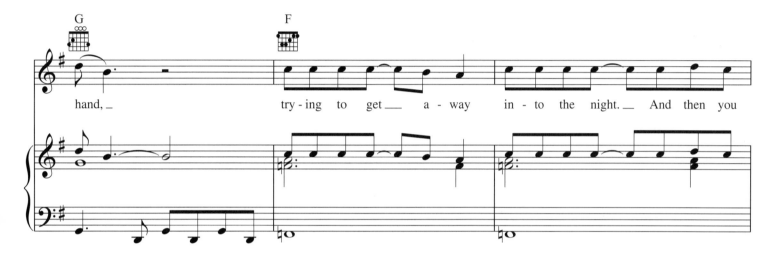

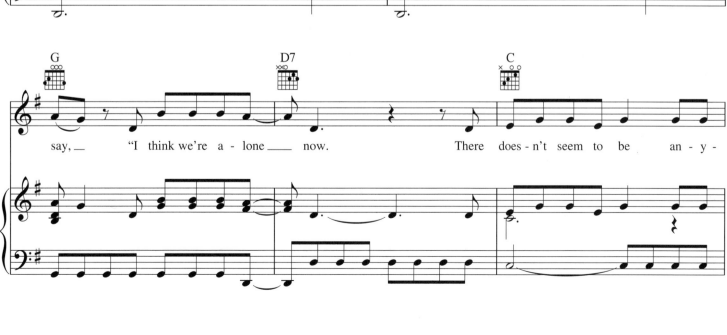

one a - round. ____ I think we're a - lone ____ now. The

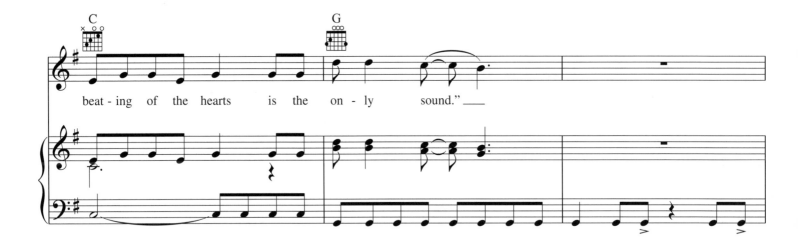

beat - ing of the hearts is the on - ly sound." ____

"I think we're a - lone ____ now. The

Repeat and Fade **Optional Ending**

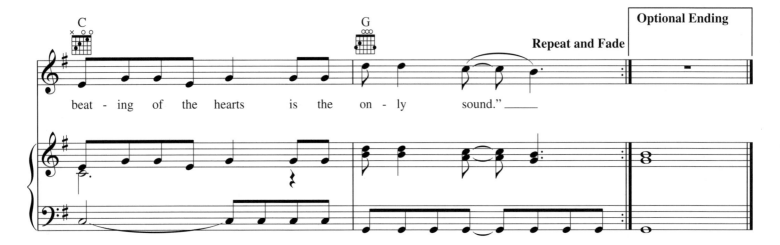

beat - ing of the hearts is the on - ly sound." ____

IF LOVING YOU IS WRONG
I DON'T WANT TO BE RIGHT

Words and Music by HOMER BANKS,
CARL HAMPTON and RAYMOND JACKSON

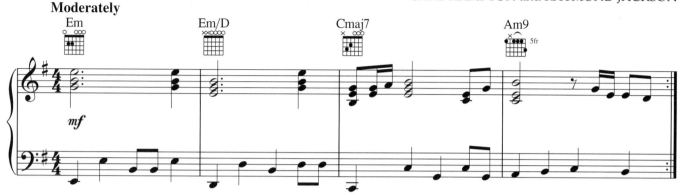

If lov-in' you is wrong, I don't want to be right. If
Am I wrong to fall so deep-ly in love with you,

be-ing right_ means be-ing with-out_ you, I'd rath-er live a wrong-do-ing life. Your
know-ing I got a wife and two lit-tle chil-dren de-pend-ing on me, too? But

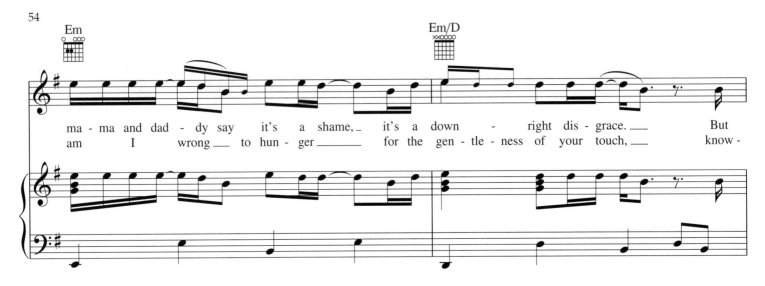

ma - ma and dad - dy say it's a shame,_ it's a down - right dis - grace._ But
am I wrong_ to hun - ger _____ for the gen - tle - ness of your touch, ___ know -

long as I got you by my side_ I don't care what your peo - ple say. _____ Your
ing I got some - one else at home ___ who needs me just as much. ___ And

friends tell you it's _ no fu - ture in lov - ing a mar - ried man. _ If
are you wrong to give your love to a mar - ried man? _ And

I can't see you when I want _ to I'll see you when_ I can. _____ If
am I wrong for try - ing to hold on to the best thing I ev - er had? _

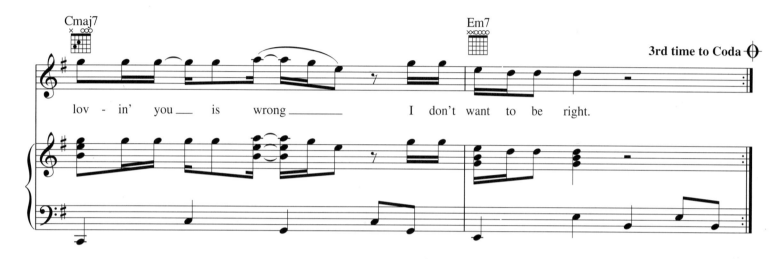

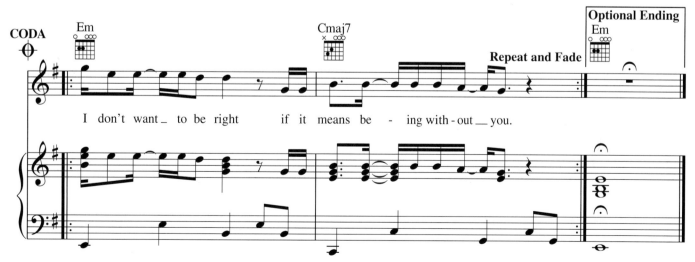

56

I'LL BE SATISFIED

Words and Music by BERRY GORDY,
GWEN GORDY FUQUA and TYRAN CARLO

With a beat

IKO IKO

Words and Music by ROSA LEE HAWKINS,
BARBARA ANN HAWKINS, JOAN MARIE JOHNSON, JOE JONES,
MARALYN JONES, SHARON JONES and JESSIE THOMAS

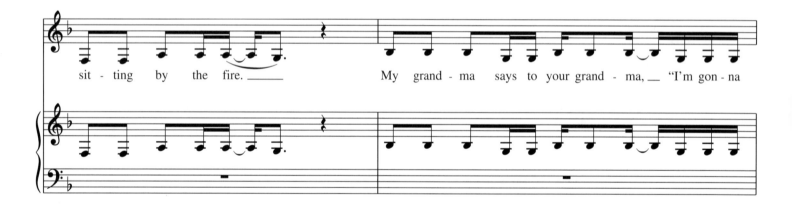

59

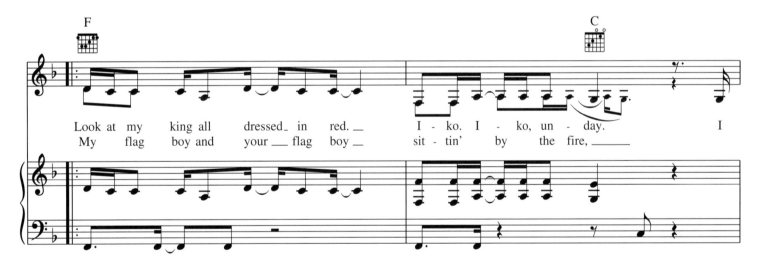

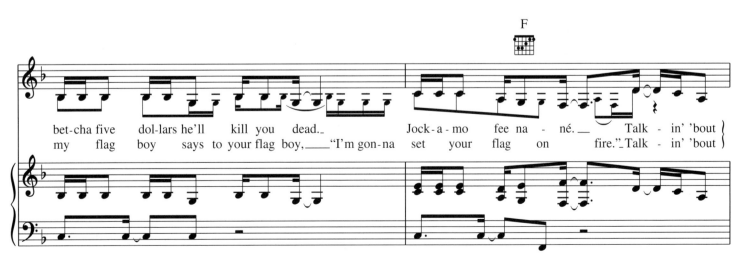

hey now! (hey now) Hey now! (hey __ now) I - ko. I - ko, un - day.

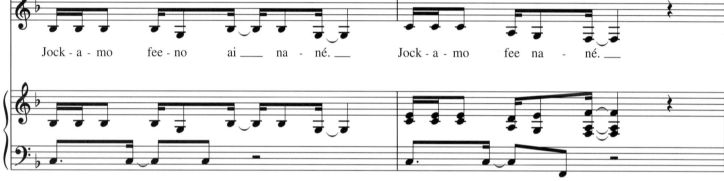

Jock - a - mo fee - no ai __ na - né. __ Jock - a - mo fee na - né. __

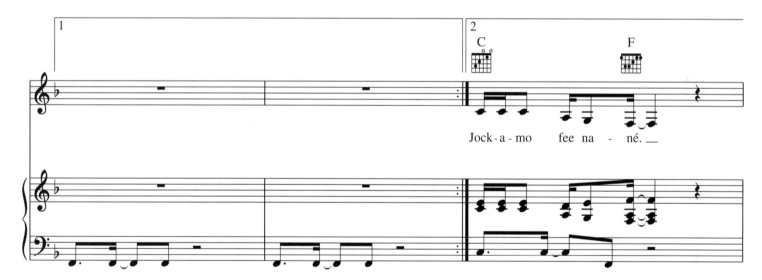

Jock - a - mo fee na - né. __

He's not a man; he's a lov-in' ma-chine. __ Jock-a-mo fee na - né. __ Talk - in' 'bout

hey now! (hey now) Hey now! (hey __ now) I - ko. I - ko, un - day.

Jock-a-mo fee-no ai __ na - né. __ Jock-a-mo fee na - né. __ Talk - in' 'bout

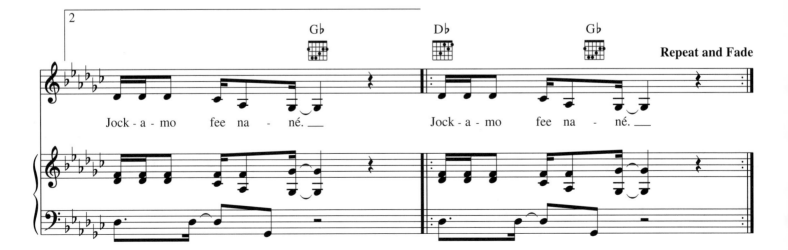

Repeat and Fade

Jock-a-mo fee na - né. __ Jock-a-mo fee na - né. __

IN MY ROOM

Words and Music by BRIAN WILSON
and GARY USHER

Moderately slow

There's a world where I can go and
In this world I lock out all my
Now it's dark and I'm a - lone but

tell my se - crets to,
wor - ries and my fears,
I won't be a - fraid,
in __ my

room, __
in __ my

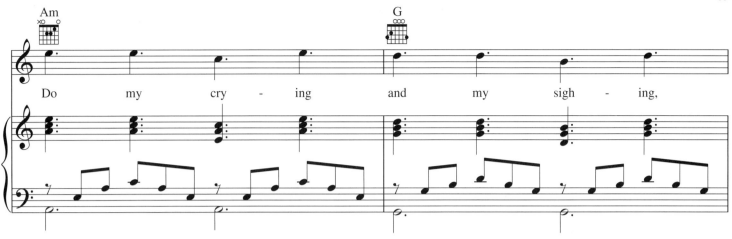

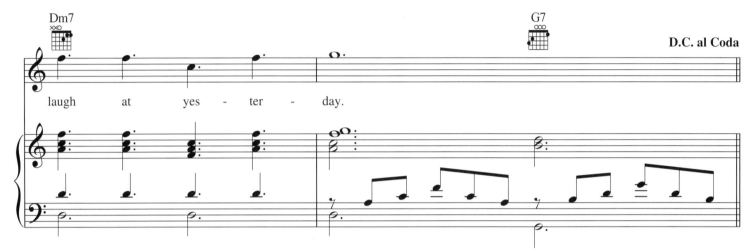

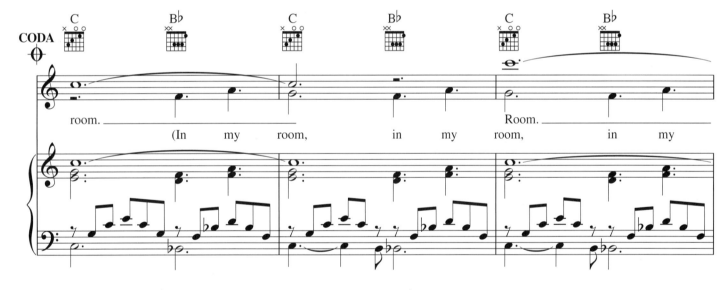

IN THE MIDNIGHT HOUR

Words and Music by STEVE CROPPER
and WILSON PICKETT

hold you, and do all the things I told you in the mid-night

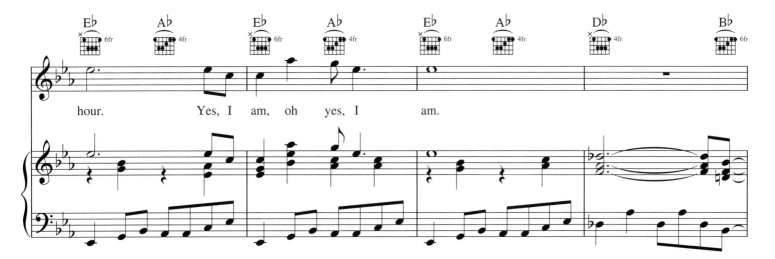

hour. Yes, I am, oh yes, I am.

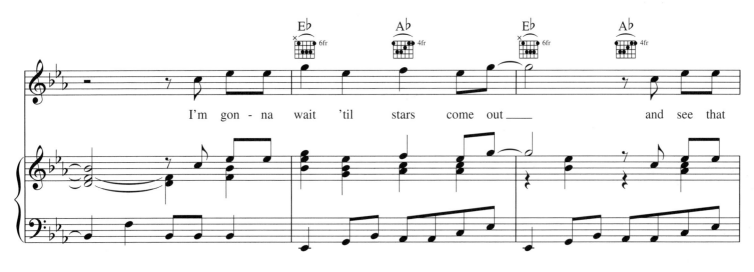

I'm gon-na wait 'til stars come out ___ and see that

twin-kle in your eyes. I'm gon-na wait 'til the mid-night hour, that's when my

love be - gins to shine. ___ You'll be the on - ly girl I'll love, ___ and

real - ly love you so in the mid - night hour, oh yeah, in the mid - night

hour. I'm gon - na hour. I'm gon - na

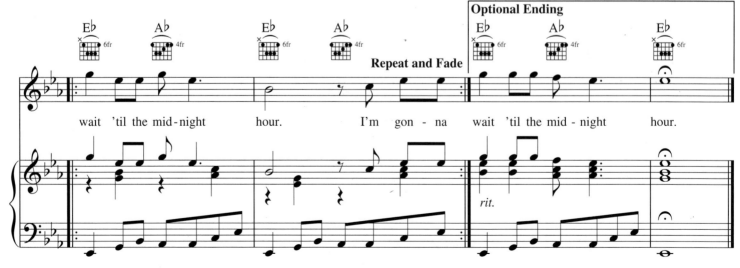

wait 'til the mid - night hour. I'm gon - na wait 'til the mid - night hour.

JOY TO THE WORLD

Words and Music by
HOYT AXTON

INDIAN RESERVATION

Words and Music by
JOHN D. LOUDERMILK

hawk and the bow _ and knife. Took a - way our na - tive

tongue, Taught their Eng - lish to ___ our

young. ___ And all the

beads we made by hand Are now - a - days made in Ja -

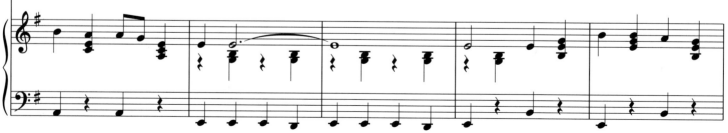

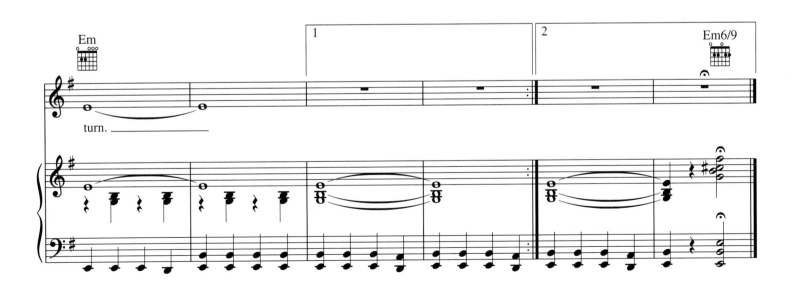

KNOCK ON WOOD

Words and Music by EDDIE FLOYD
and STEVE CROPPER

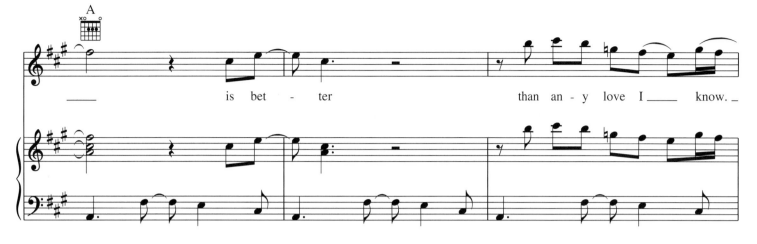

is bet - ter   than an - y love I___ know. __

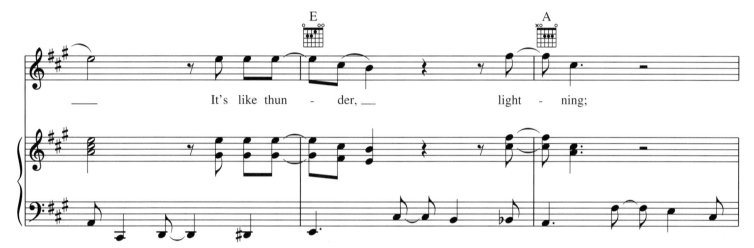

It's like thun - der, __   light - ning;

the way you love me is fright - 'ning   I think I bet - ter knock knock knock knock knock on wood.

To Coda ⊕

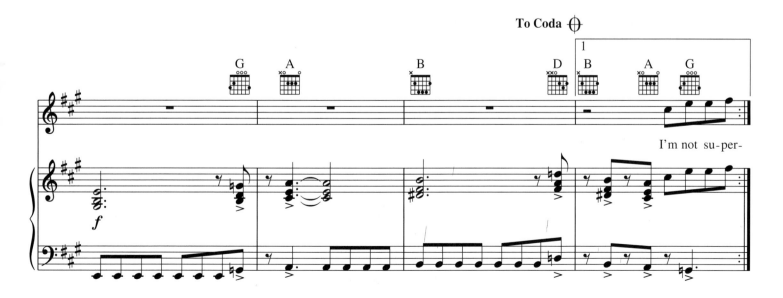

I'm not su-per-

78

D.S. al Coda

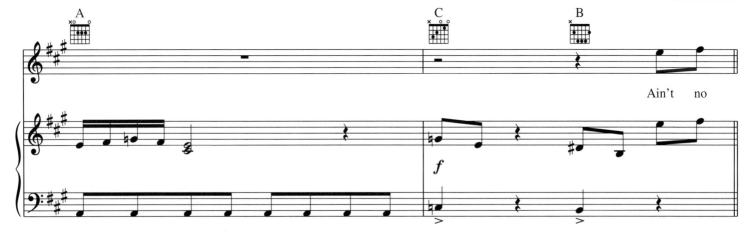

Ain't   no

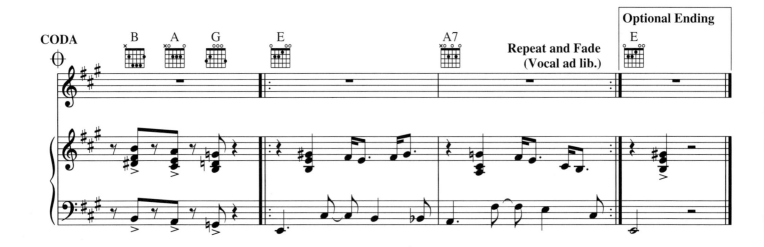

Additional Lyrics

3. Ain't no secret that a woman can feel my love come up.
You got me seeing, she really sees that, that I get enough.
Just one touch from you, baby, you know it means so much.
It's like thunder, lightning;
The way you love me is frightening,
I think I better knock-knock-knock-knock on wood.

LET'S GET TOGETHER

Words and Music by
CHET POWERS

1. Love is but the song we sing, and fear's the way we
2. Some will come and some will go, and we shall sure - ly
3. If you heard the song I sing, you must un - der-

die._____
pass._____
stand._____
You can make the
When the one who
You hold ___ the ___

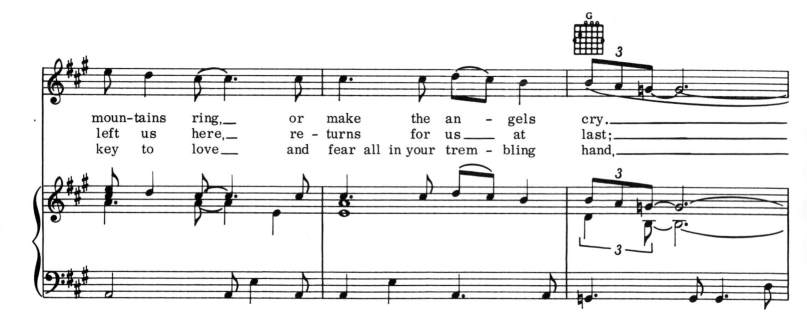

moun-tains ring,___ or make the an - gels cry._____
left us here,___ re - turns for us___ at last;_____
key to love___ and fear all in your trem - bling hand,_____

___ Know the dove is on the wing,___ and
___ We are but a mo - ments sun - light,
___ One key___ un - locks them both you know and

LET'S STAY TOGETHER

Words and Music by AL GREEN,
WILLIE MITCHELL and AL JACKSON, JR.

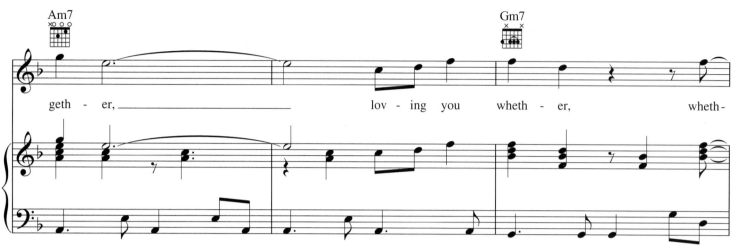

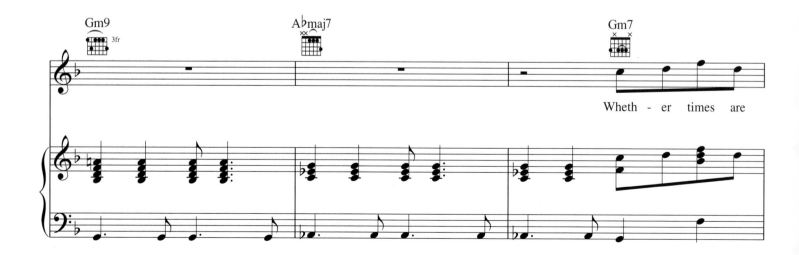

good or bad, __ hap - py or sad. ____

It's why I want us to:

Let's _____ let's stay to - geth - er, _____

__ lov - ing you wheth - er, wheth - er times are

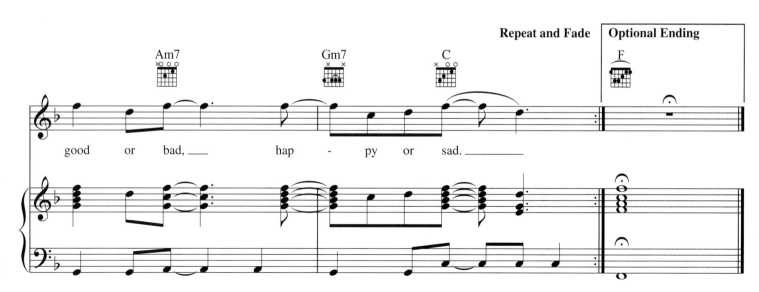

good or bad, ___ hap - py or sad. _____

LIL' RED RIDING HOOD

Words and Music by
RONALD BLACKWELL

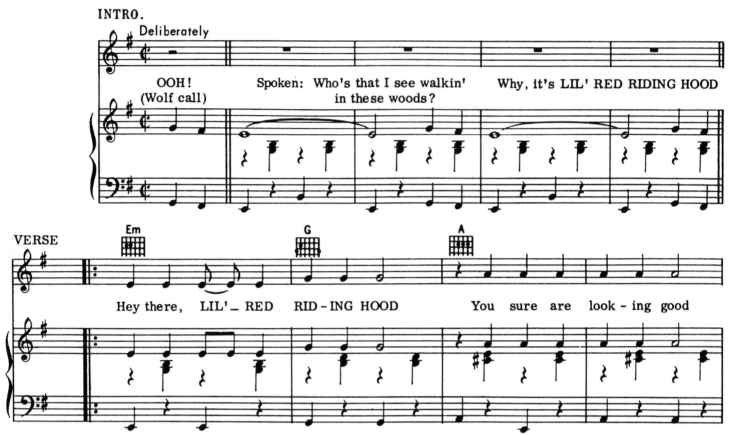

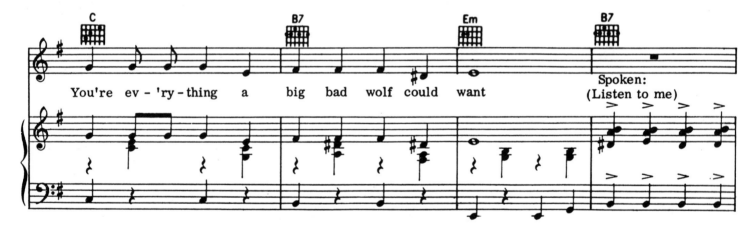

2nd Verse

I'm Gonna keep my sheep suit on
Until I'm sure that you've been shown
That I can be trusted walkin' with you alone
*OOH! LIL' RED RIDING HOOD
I'd like to hold you if I could
But you might think I'm a big bad wolf so I won't

2nd Chorus

OOH! What a big heart I have
The better to love you with
LIL' RED RIDING HOOD, even bad wolves can be good
*OOH! I'll try to be satisfied
Just to walk close by your side
Maybe you'll see things my way
Before we get to grandma's place
*Hey there, LIL' RED RIDING HOOD
You sure are looking good
You're everything that a big bad wolf could want

THE NAME GAME

By LINCOLN CHASE
and SHIRLEY ELLISTON

With a bright beat

The name ___ game. ___

Shir-ley!
Shir-ley, Shir-ley, bo-ber-ley, bo - na - na fan-na fo-fer-ley,
Lin-coln!
Lin-coln, Lin-coln, bo-bin-coln, bo - na - na fan-na fo-fln-coln,

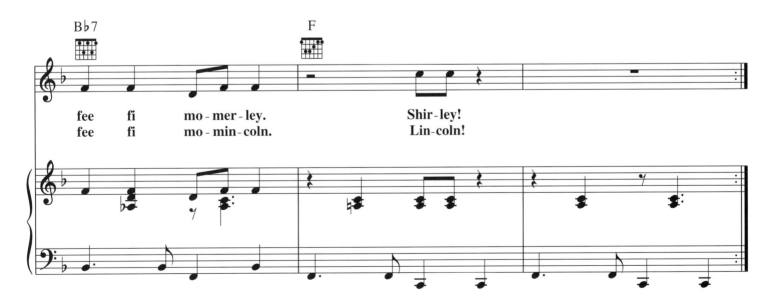

fee fi mo-mer-ley.
Shir-ley!
fee fi mo-min-coln.
Lin-coln!

LOUIE, LOUIE

Words and Music by
RICHARD BERRY

Medium Rock beat

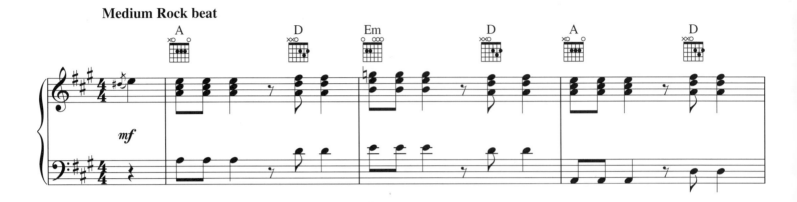

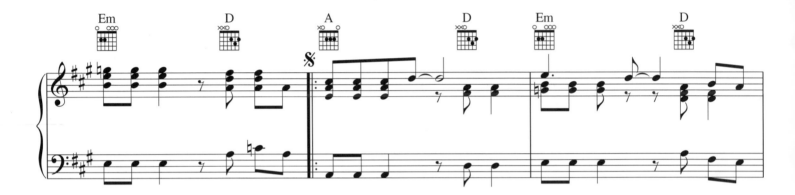

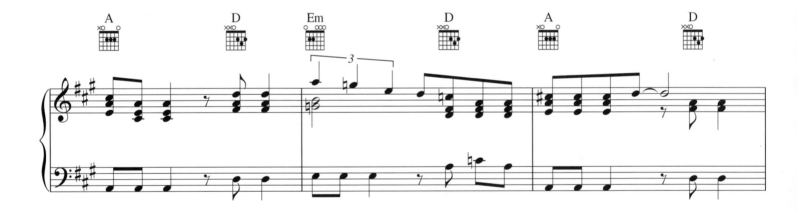

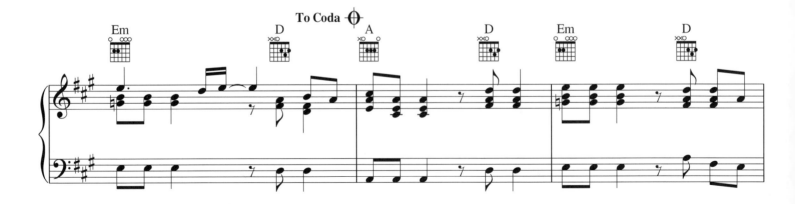

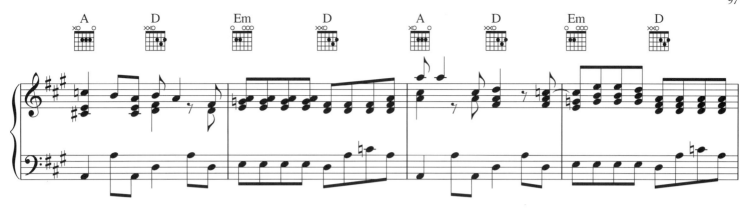

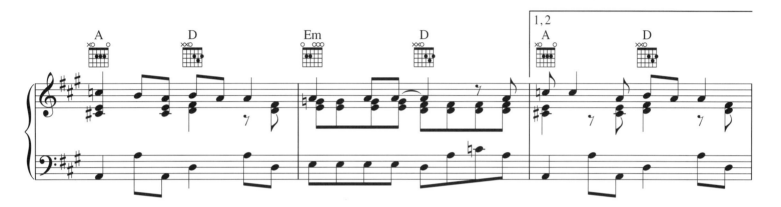

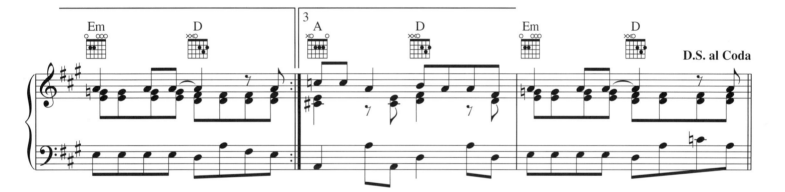

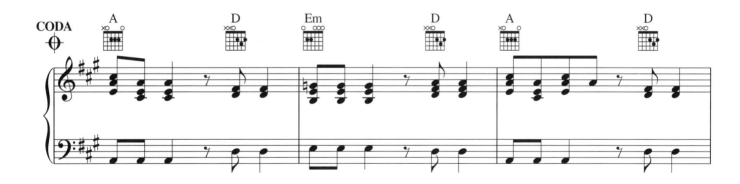

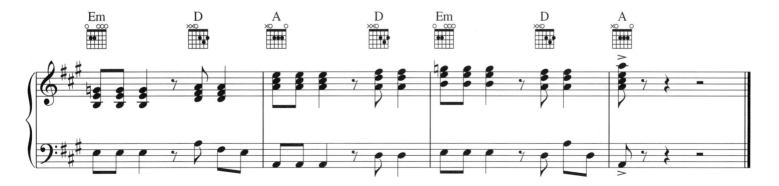

NIGHTS IN WHITE SATIN

Words and Music by
JUSTIN HAYWARD

NOBODY BUT ME

Words and Music by RUDOLPH ISLEY,
RONALD ISLEY and O'KELLY ISLEY

skate like I do. __ No - bod - y can do the boog - a - loo like I do. __ No - bod - y can do the

phil - ly like I do. __ Well, don't you know I've got a fish I do, ain't __ no - bod - y do it but

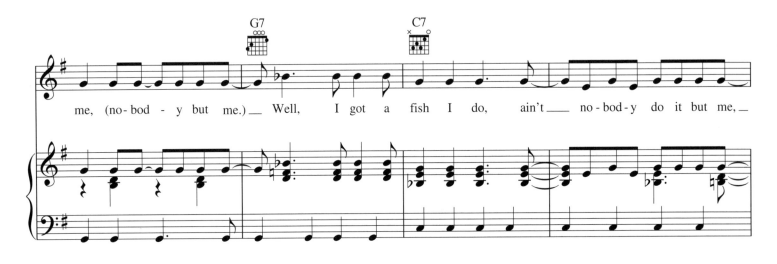

me, (no - bod - y but me.) __ Well, I got a fish I do, ain't __ no - bod - y do it but me, __

__ babe. (No - bod - y but me.) __ Well, let me tell ya no - bod - y, but no - bod - y but

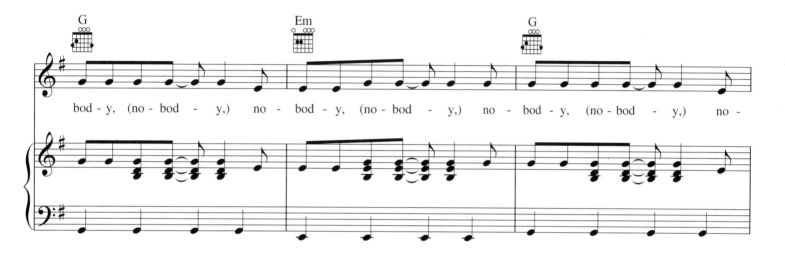

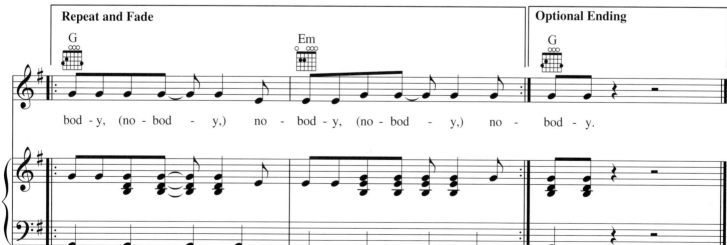

(You've Got)
PERSONALITY

Words and Music by LLOYD PRICE
and HAROLD LOGAN

RESPECT

Words and Music by
OTIS REDDING

ROCK YOUR BABY

Words and Music by HARRY WAYNE CASEY
and RICHARD FINCH

(Spoken:) Sexy ...

SHOUT

Words and Music by O'KELLY ISLEY,
RONALD ISLEY and RUDOLPH ISLEY

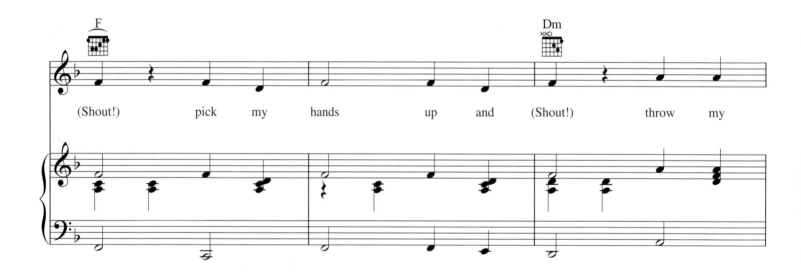

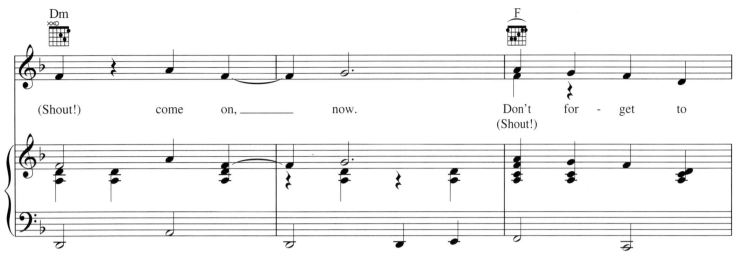

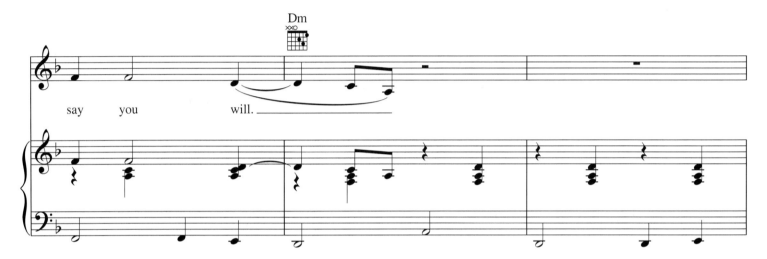

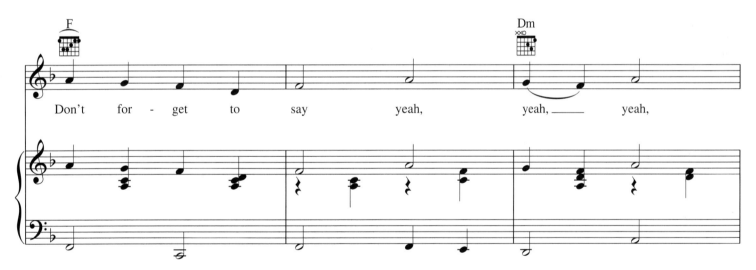

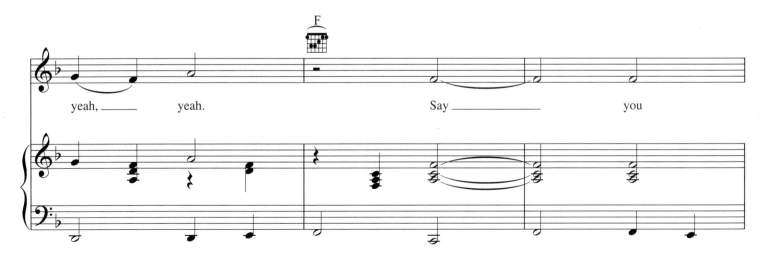

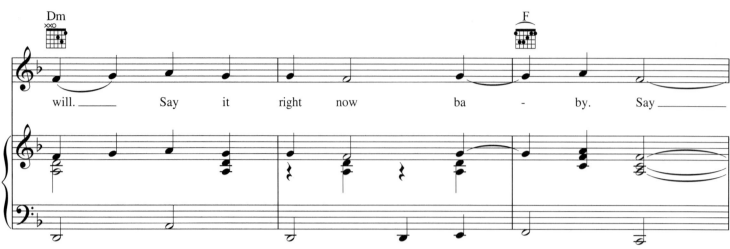

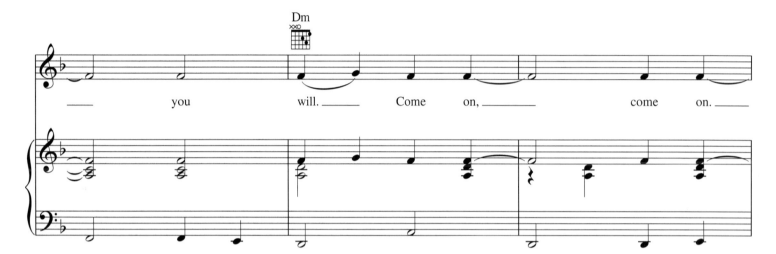

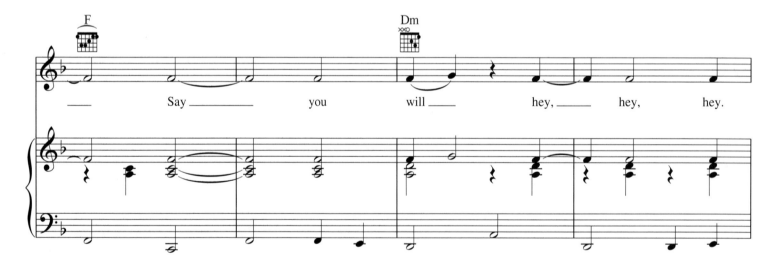

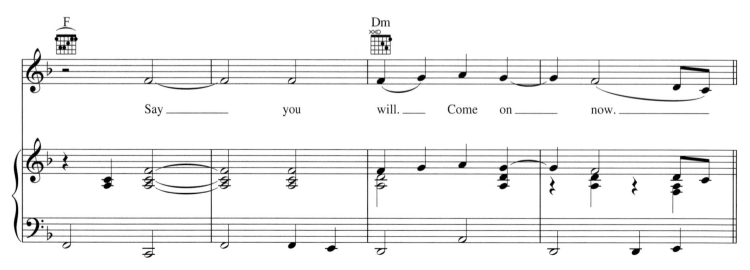

117

(Say) Say that you love me. (Say) Say that you
(Say) Say that you want me. (Say) Say You wan-na

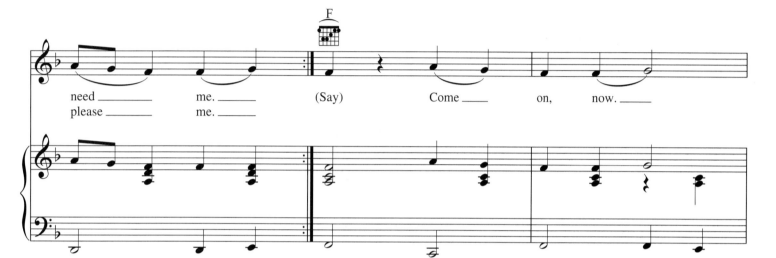

need _____ me. _____ (Say) Come ____ on, now. _____
please _____ me. _____

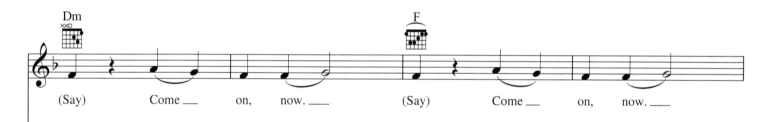

(Say) Come ____ on, now. ____ (Say) Come ____ on, now. ____

(Say.) I still re - mem - ber

(Shoo - by

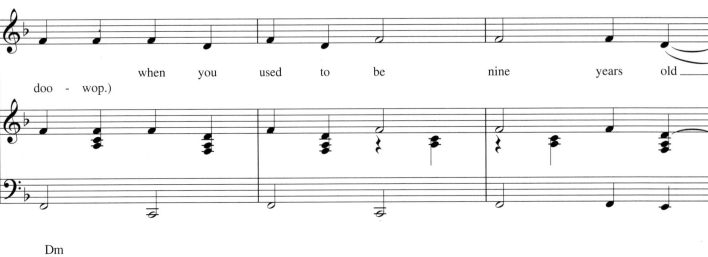

when you used to be nine years old ____

doo - wop.)

(Shoo - by - doo.)

yeah, ____ yeah. ____

I was a fool ____ for you from the

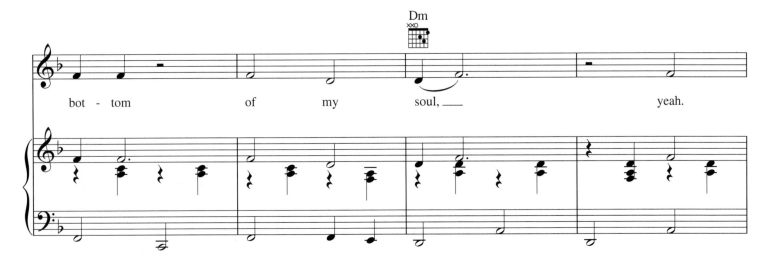

bot - tom of my soul, ____ yeah.

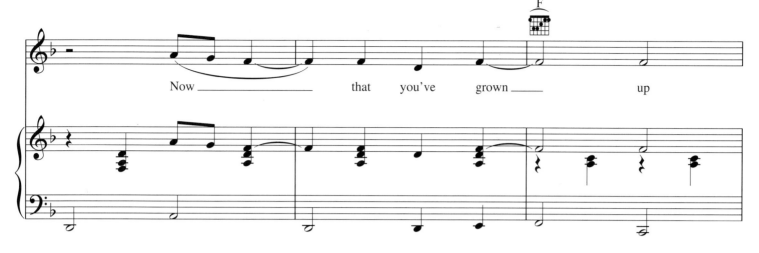

Now _____ that you've grown _____ up

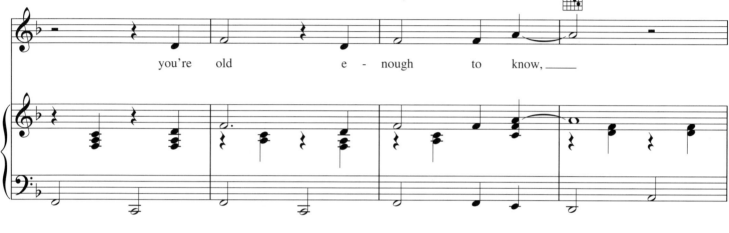

you're old e - nough to know, _____

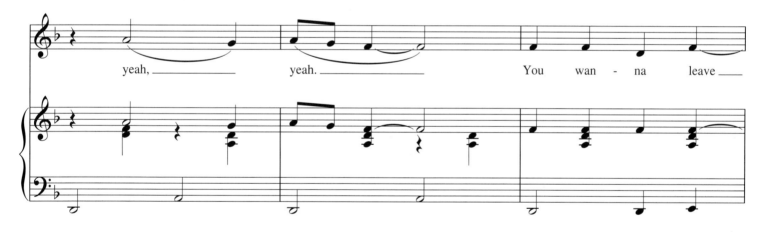

yeah, _____ yeah. _____ You wan - na leave _____

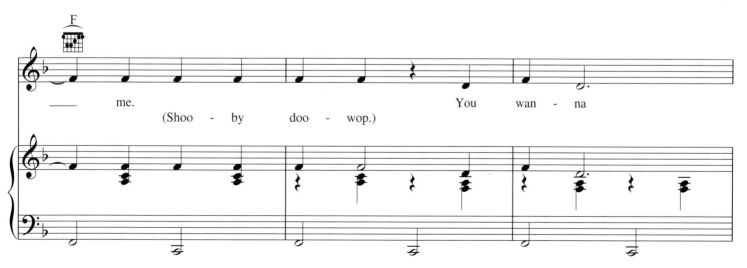

_____ me. You wan - na
(Shoo - by doo - wop.)

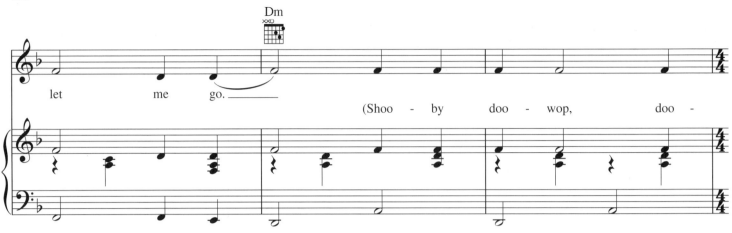

let me go. _____ (Shoo - by doo - wop, doo -

Swing

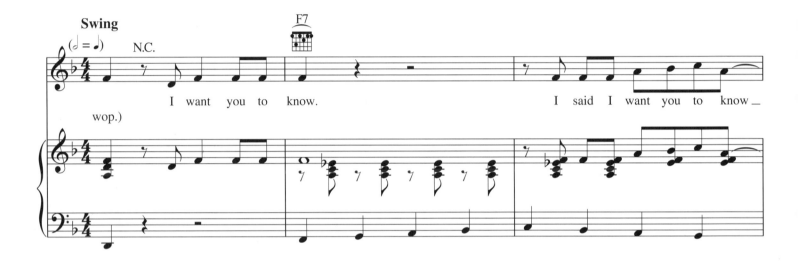

I want you to know. I said I want you to know _

wop.)

_ right now, yeah. You've been good _ to me ba - by, _____

bet - ter than I've been to my - self, yeah, hey. And if you ev - er

leave _____ me __ I don't want no - bod - y else, hey, hey.

I said I want you to know, _____ hey. I said I want you to know __

Original Tempo
($\quad = \quad$)

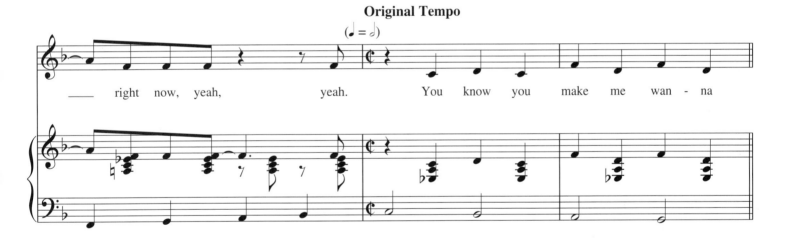

__ right now, yeah, yeah. You know you make me wan - na

F   **Dm**

Play 7 times

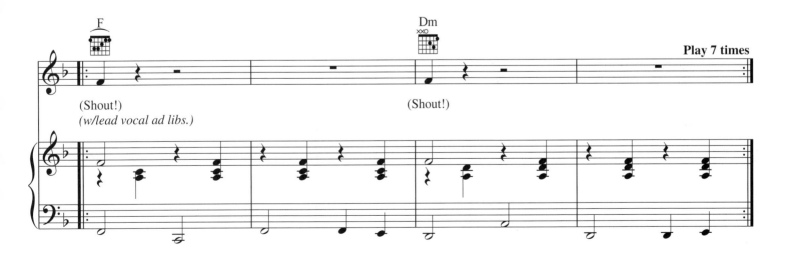

(Shout!)   (Shout!)
(w/lead vocal ad libs.)

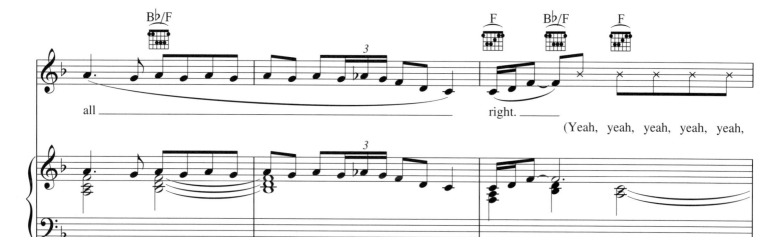

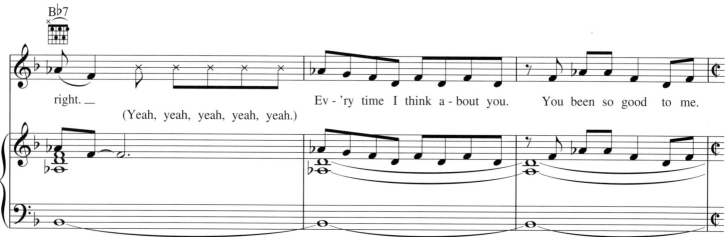

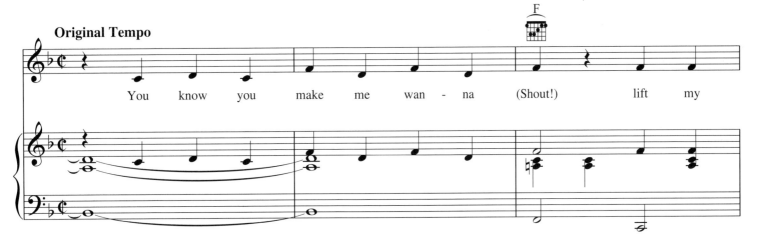

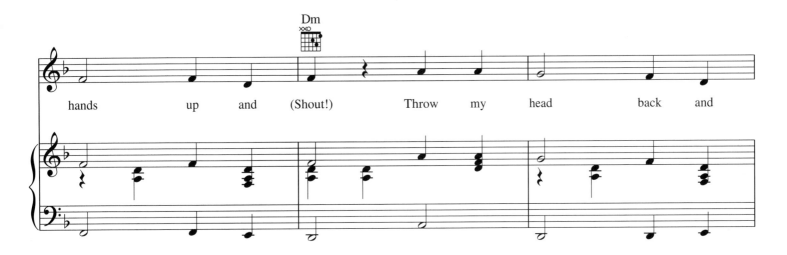

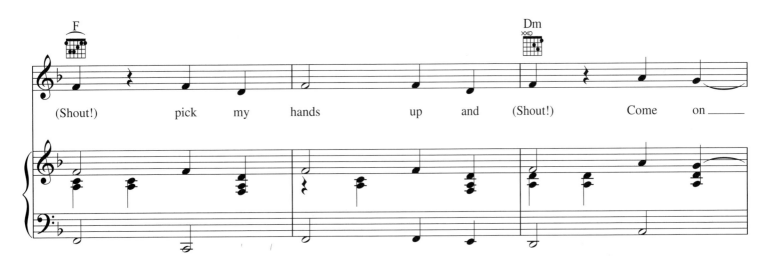

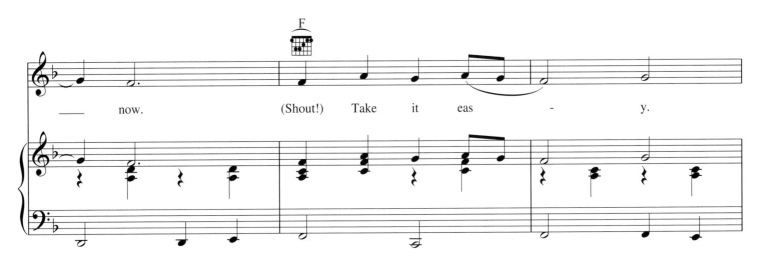

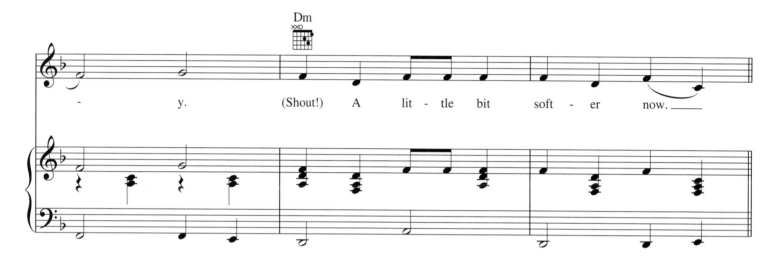

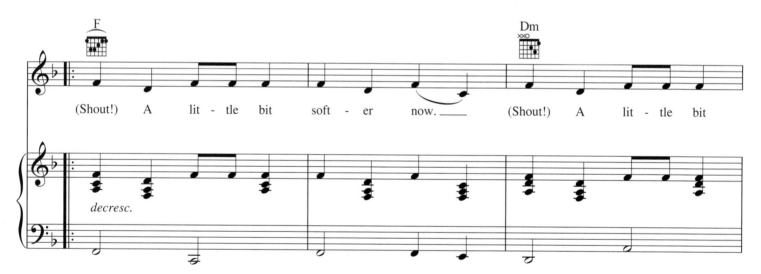

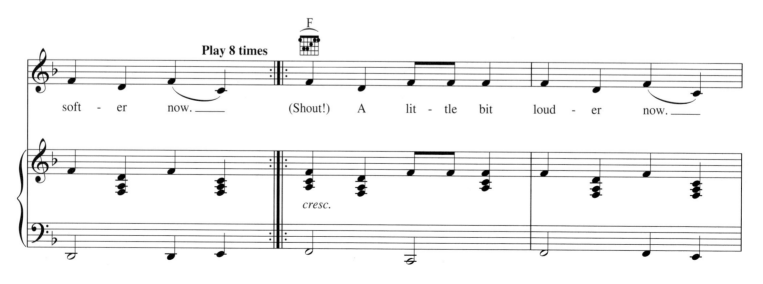

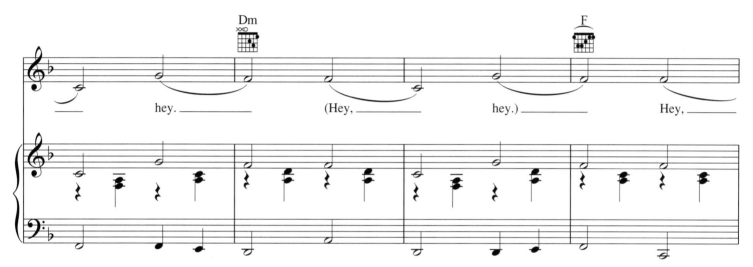

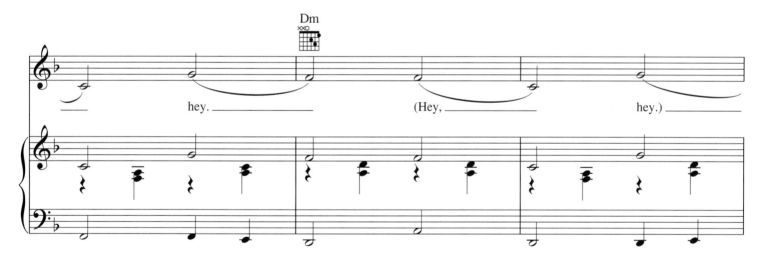

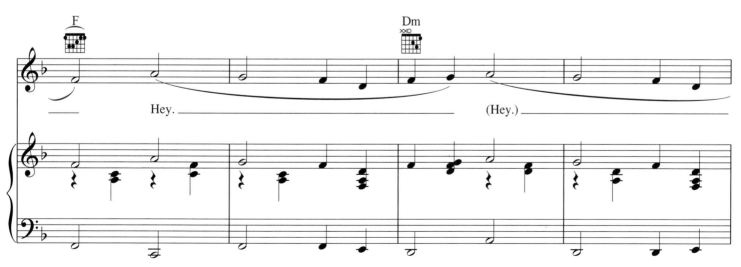

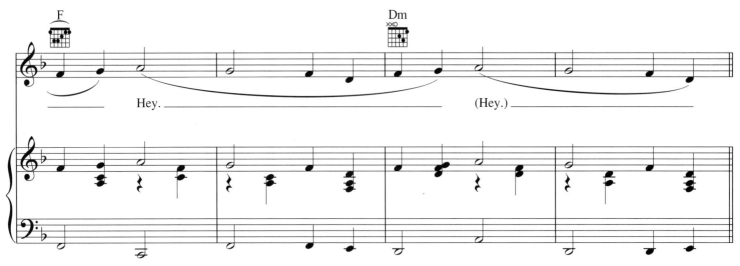

Hey. (Hey.)

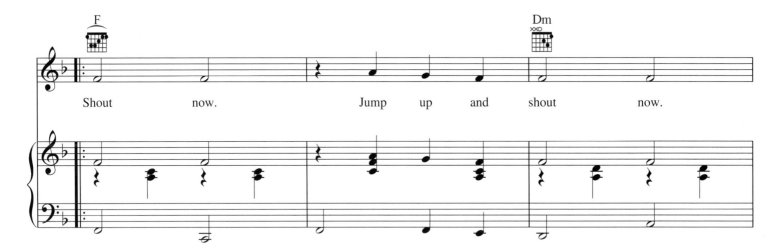

Shout now. Jump up and shout now.

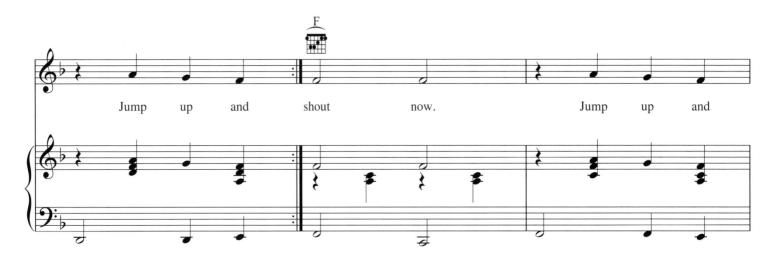

Jump up and shout now. Jump up and

shout now. Ev - 'ry - bod - y shout now.

SIGNS

Words and Music by
LES EMMERSON

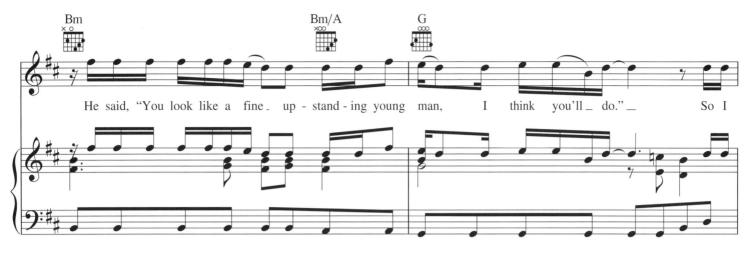

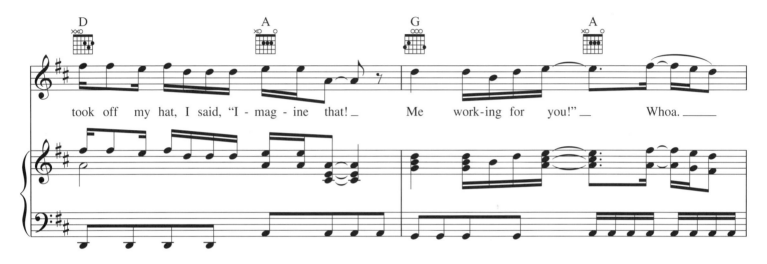

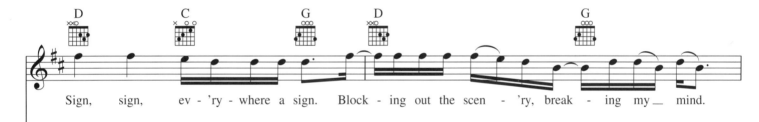

Now, hey you, mis - ter, can't you read? You've

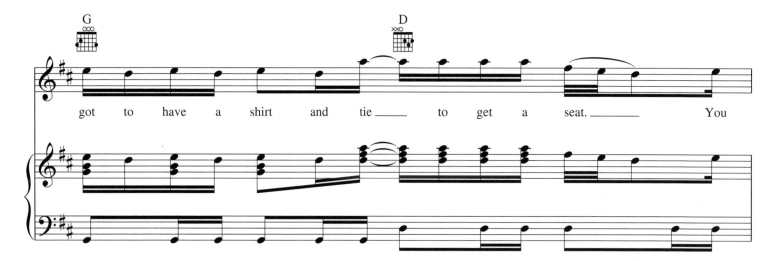

got to have a shirt and tie to get a seat. You

can't e - ven watch. No, you can't eat. You ain't sup - posed to

be here.

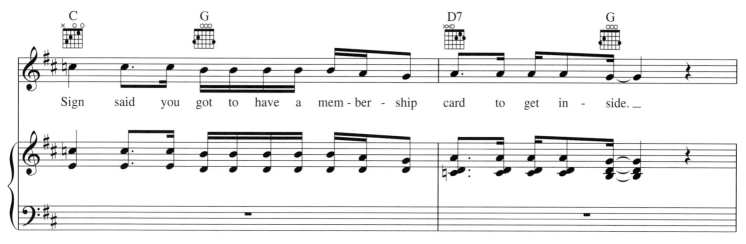

Sign said you got to have a mem-ber-ship card to get in - side. __

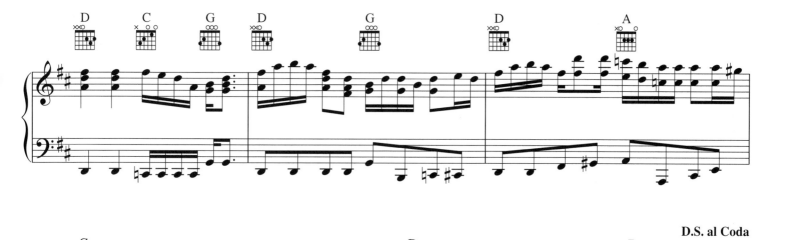

D.S. al Coda

And the

CODA

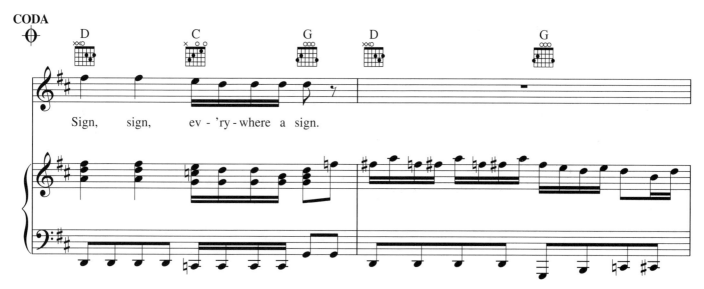

Sign, sign, ev - 'ry-where a sign.

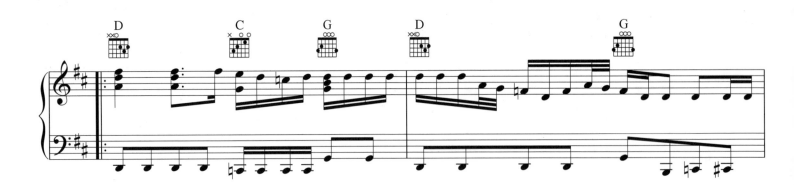

SINCERELY

Words and Music by ALAN FREED
and HARVEY FUQUA

(Sittin' On)
THE DOCK OF THE BAY

Words and Music by STEVE CROPPER
and OTIS REDDING

Looks like noth-in's gon-na change;___ ev - 'ry-thing

still ___ re-mains the same.___ I can't do what ten peo-ple tell me ___ to do, ___

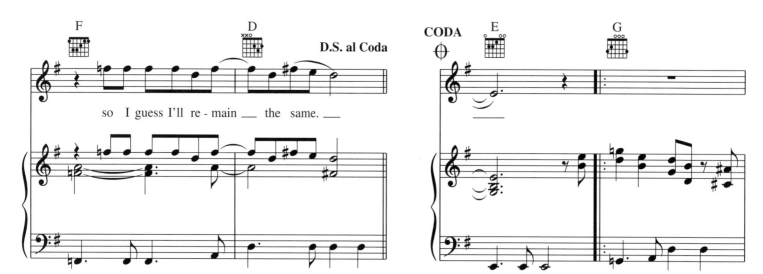

so I guess I'll re-main ___ the same. ___

D.S. al Coda

CODA

Repeat ad lib. **Optional Ending**

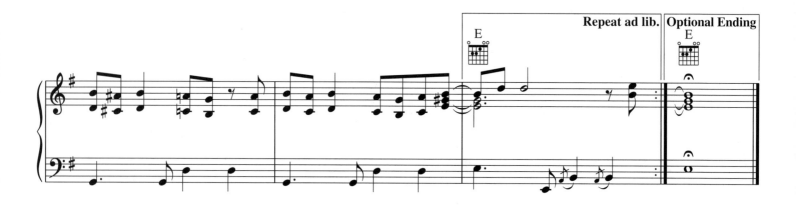

SOMEBODY TO LOVE

Words and Music by
DARBY SLICK

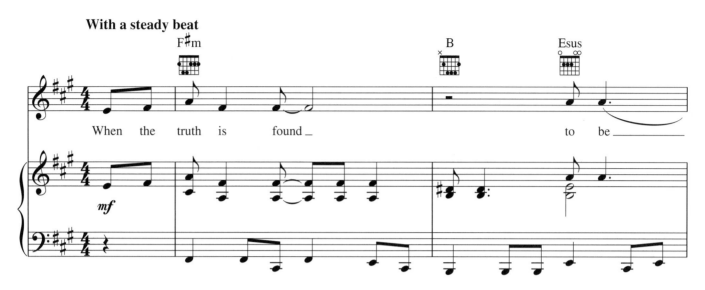

When the truth is found ___ to be ___

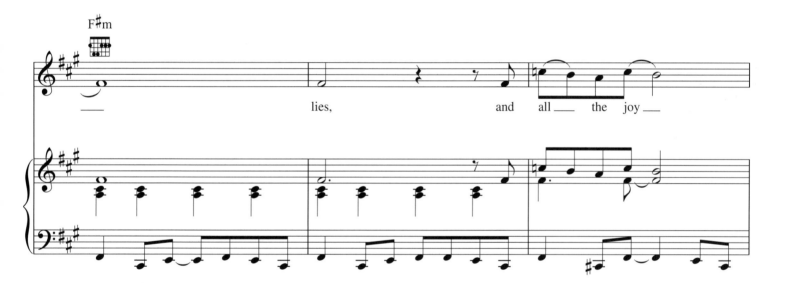

___ lies, and all ___ the joy ___

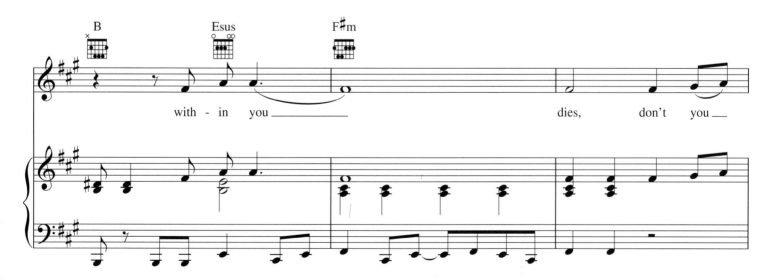

with - in you ___ dies, don't you ___

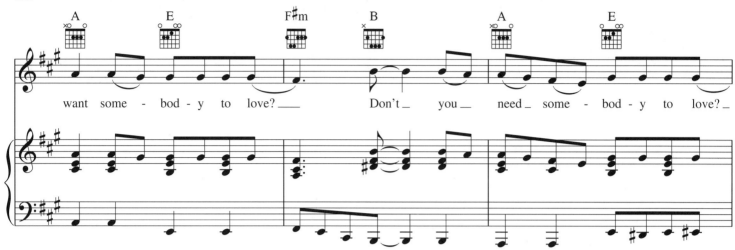

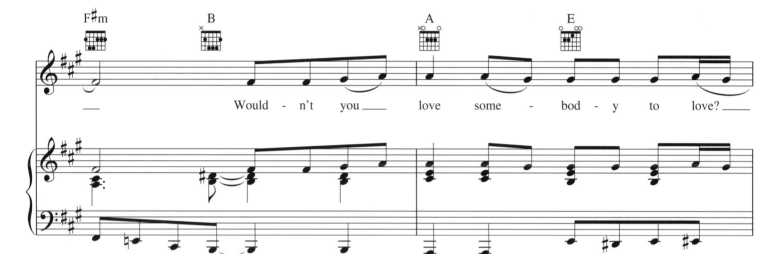

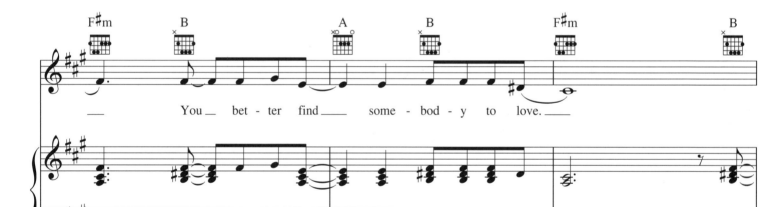

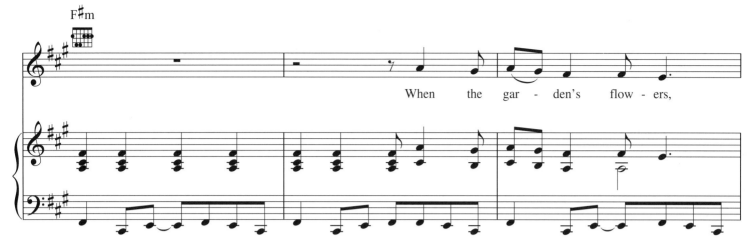

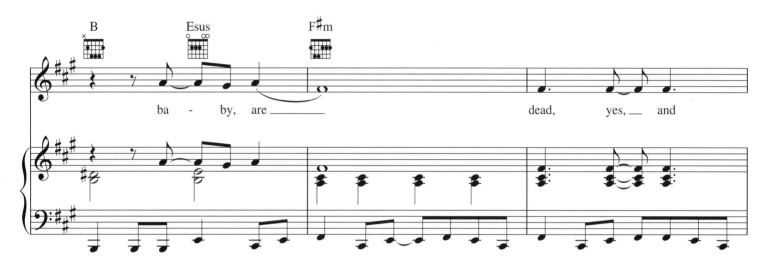

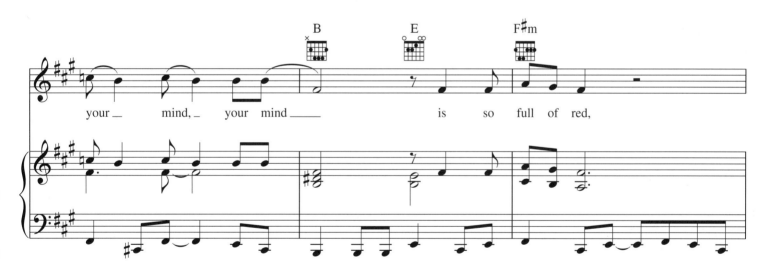

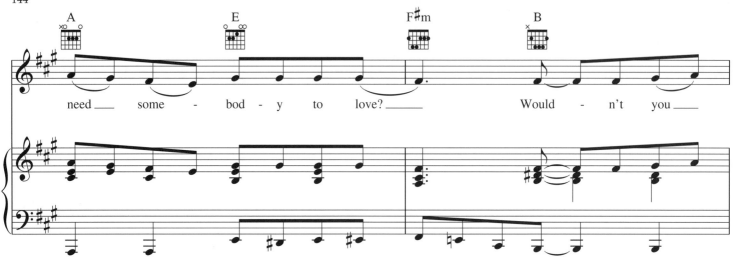

need ___ some - bod - y to love? ___ Would - n't you ___

love some - bod - y to love? ___ You ___ bet - ter find ___ some - bod - y to love. ___

Your eyes, ___ I say your eyes ___ may

look like his. ___ Yeah, but

in your head, ba - by, ___ I'm a - fraid you don't know where it is. ___

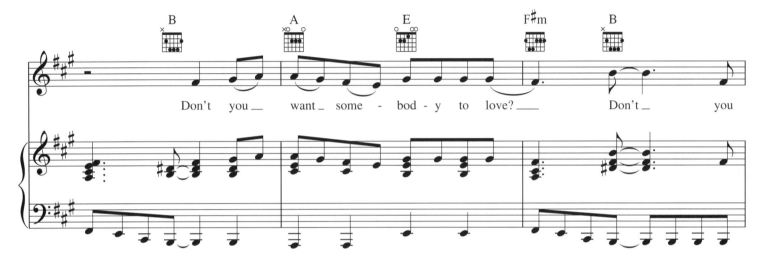

Don't you ___ want ___ some - bod - y to love? ___ Don't ___ you

need some - bod - y to love? ___ Would - n't you ___ love some - bod - y to love? _

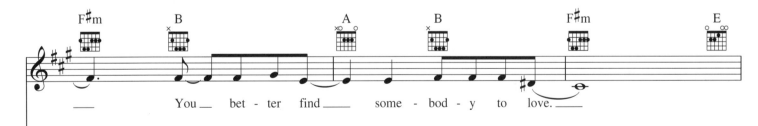

___ You ___ bet - ter find ___ some - bod - y to love. ___

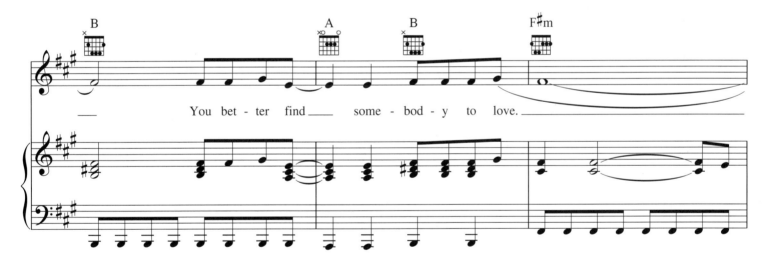

SPEEDOO

Words and Music by
ESTHER NAVARRO

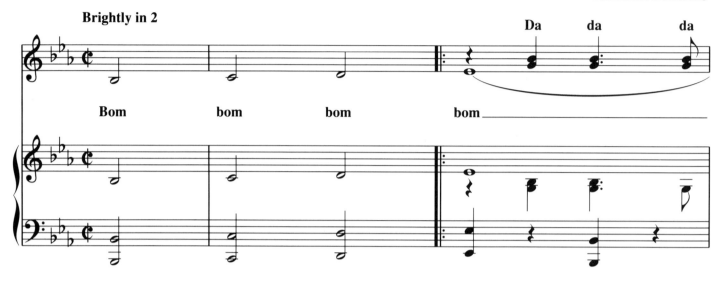

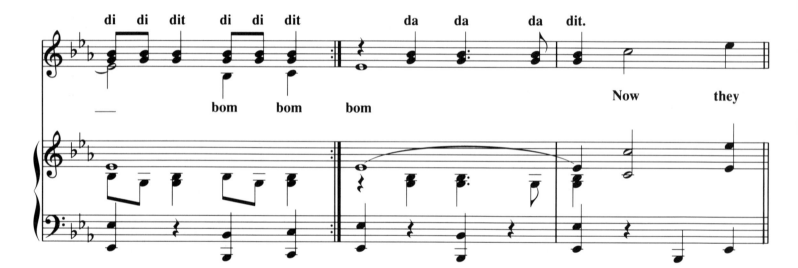

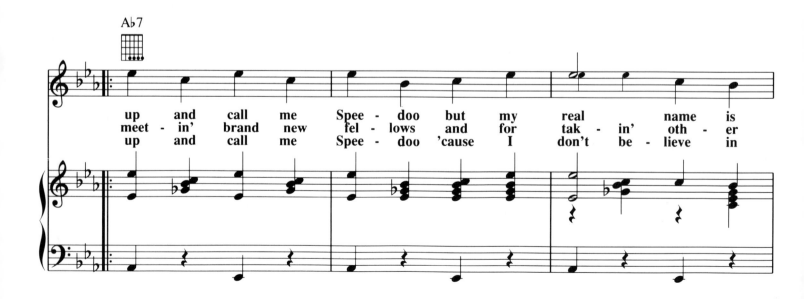

150

TEEN ANGEL

Words and Music by
JEAN SURREY

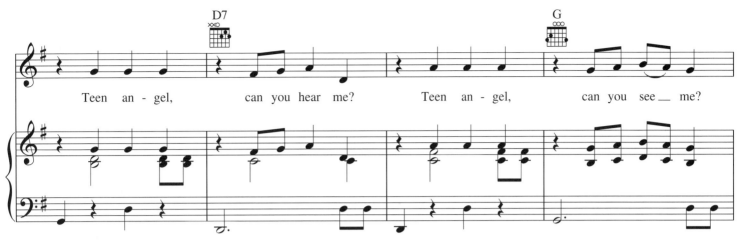

Teen an - gel, can you hear me? Teen an - gel, can you see __ me?

Are you some - where up a - bove and am I still your

own __ true love? What own __ true love?
Just

Freely

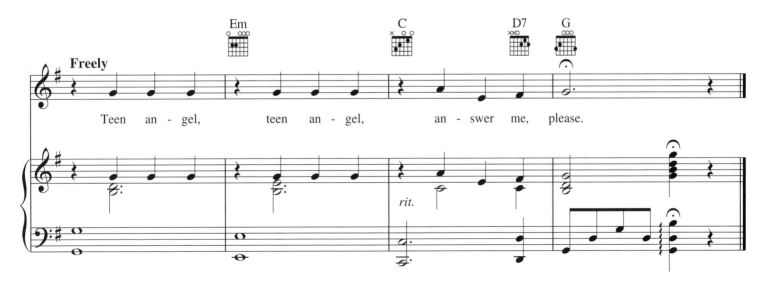

Teen an - gel, teen an - gel, an - swer me, please.

rit.

TEQUILA

By CHUCK RIO

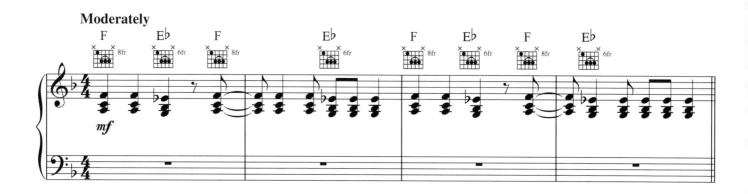

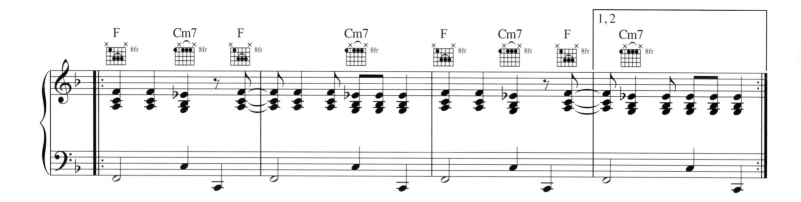

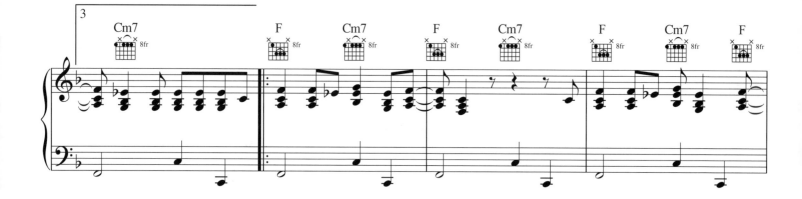

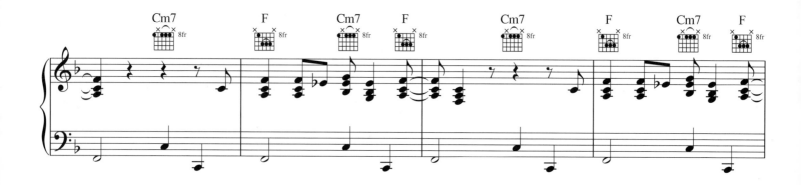

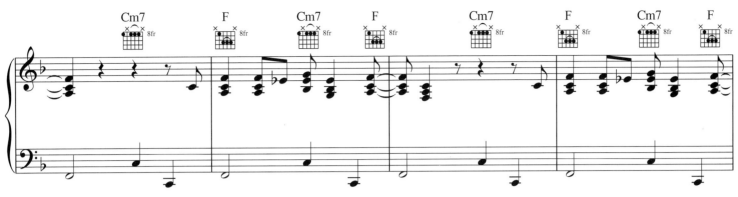

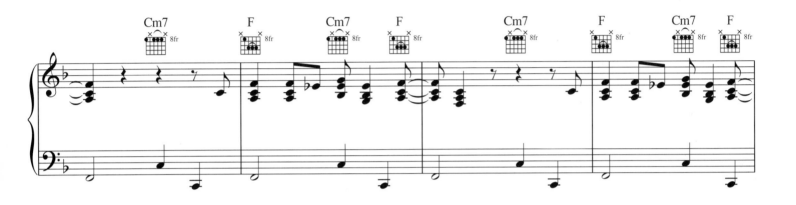

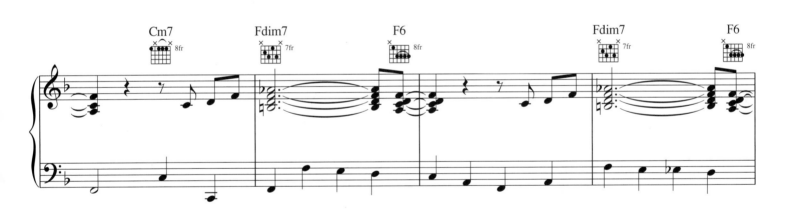

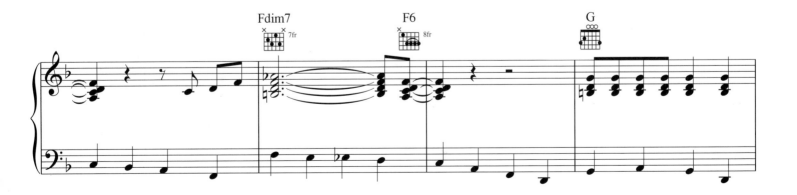

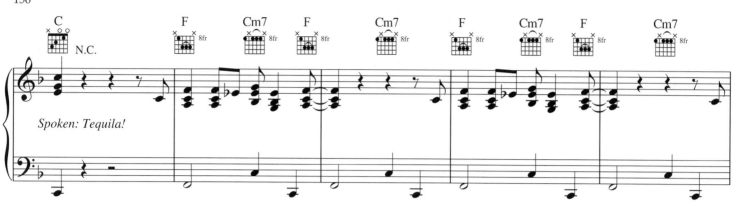

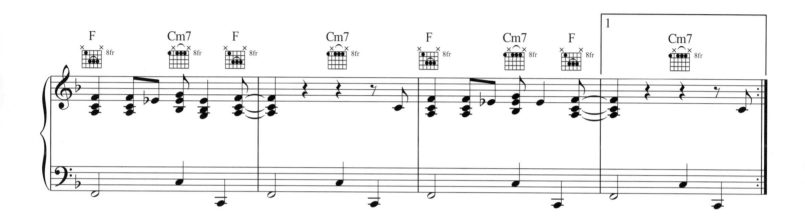

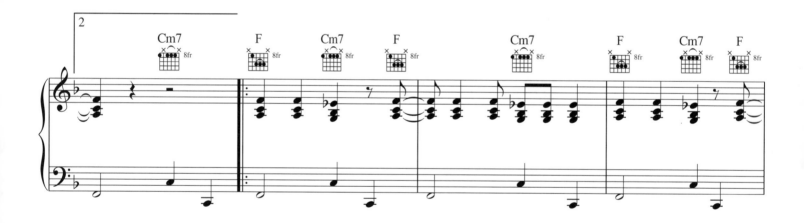

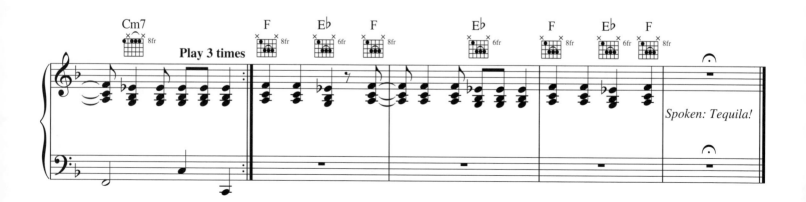

THAT'S WHEN YOUR HEARTACHES BEGIN

Words and Music by FRED FISHER,
WILLIAM RASKIN and WILLIAM J. HILL

158

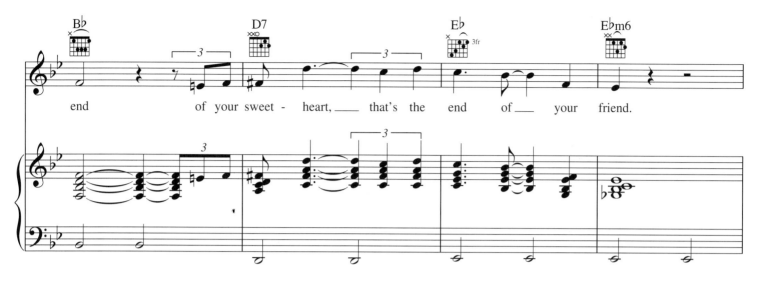

end   of your sweet - heart, ____ that's the   end   of ____ your   friend.

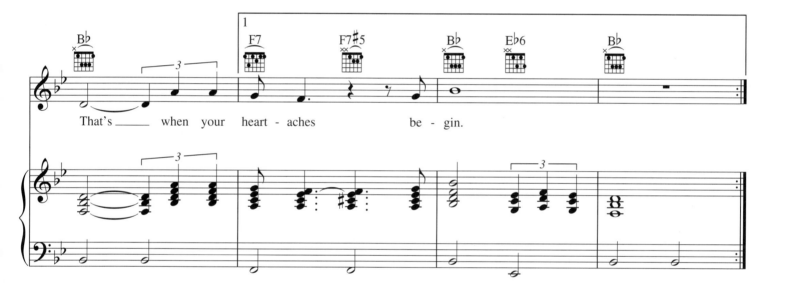

That's ____ when your heart - aches   be - gin.

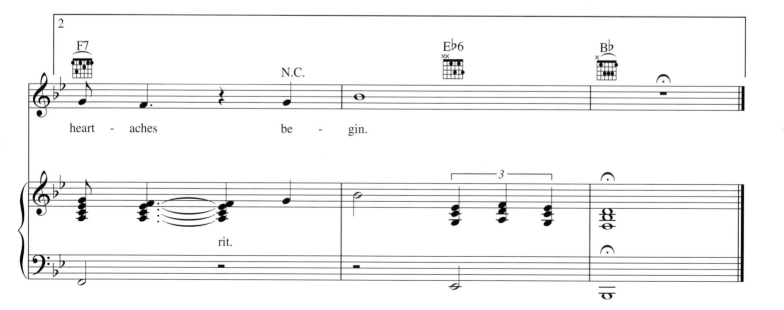

heart - aches   be - gin.

rit.

TRAVELIN' MAN

Words and Music by
JERRY FULLER

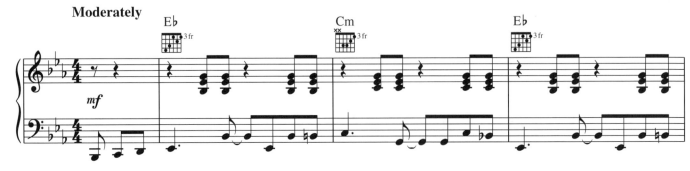

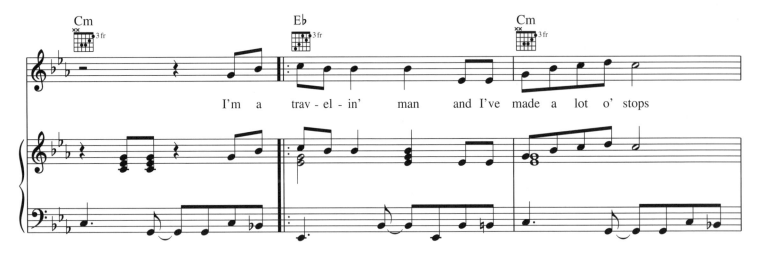

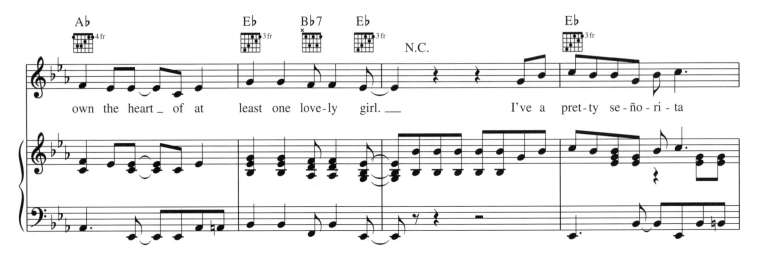

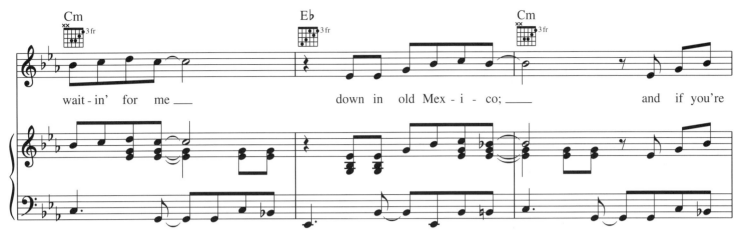

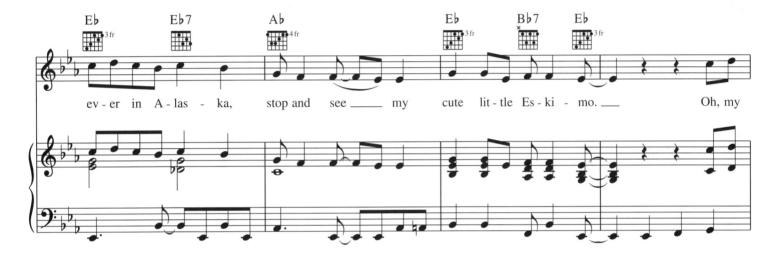

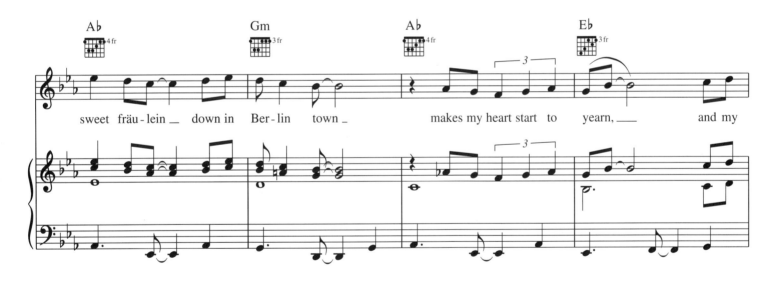

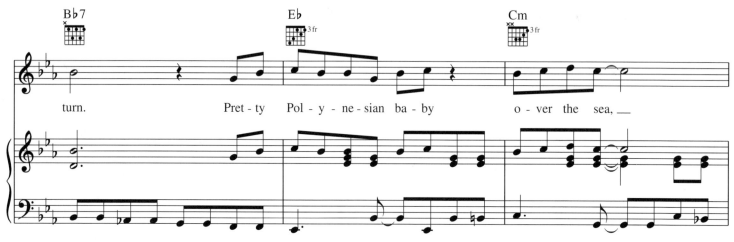

turn. Pret - ty Pol - y - ne - sian ba - by o - ver the sea, __

I re - mem - ber the night __ when we walked on the sands of

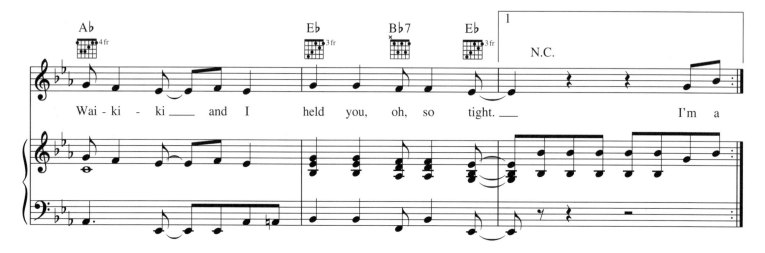

Wai - ki - ki __ and I held you, oh, so tight. __ I'm a

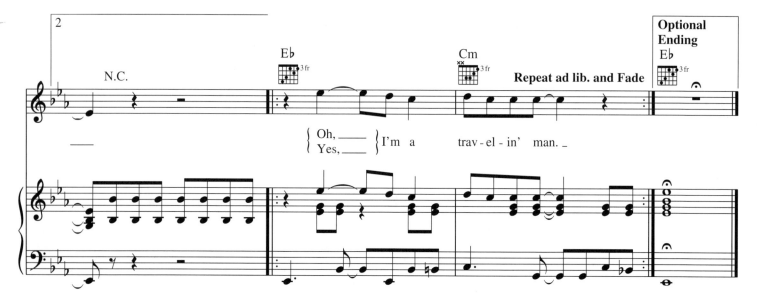

— Oh, __ / Yes, __ I'm a trav - el - in' man. _

A WHITER SHADE OF PALE

Words and Music by KEITH REID
and GARY BROOKER

WALKIN' THE DOG

Words and Music by
RUFUS THOMAS

Moderate Rock

YOUNG BLOOD

Words and Music by JERRY LEIBER,
MIKE STOLLER and DOC POMUS

I saw her stand - in' on the cor - ner,
I took one look and I was frac - tured.
I could - n't sleep a wink for try - in'.

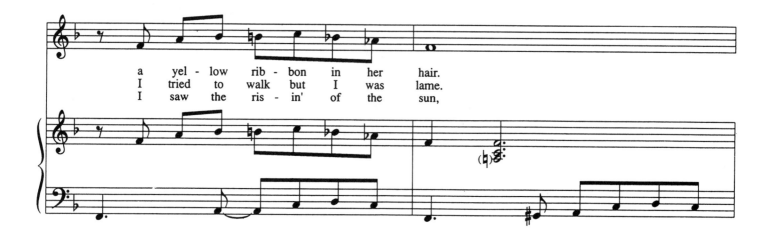

a yel - low rib - bon in her hair.
I tried to walk but I was lame.
I saw the ris - in' of the sun,

172

YOU DIDN'T HAVE TO BE SO NICE

Words and Music by JOHN SEBASTIAN
and STEVE BOONE